797,885 Books
are available to read at

Forgotten Books

www.ForgottenBooks.com

Forgotten Books' App
Available for mobile, tablet & eReader

ISBN 978-1-330-19914-5
PIBN 10050803

This book is a reproduction of an important historical work. Forgotten Books uses state-of-the-art technology to digitally reconstruct the work, preserving the original format whilst repairing imperfections present in the aged copy. In rare cases, an imperfection in the original, such as a blemish or missing page, may be replicated in our edition. We do, however, repair the vast majority of imperfections successfully; any imperfections that remain are intentionally left to preserve the state of such historical works.

Forgotten Books is a registered trademark of FB &c Ltd.
Copyright © 2017 FB &c Ltd.
FB &c Ltd, Dalton House, 60 Windsor Avenue, London, SW19 2RR.
Company number 08720141. Registered in England and Wales.

For support please visit www.forgottenbooks.com

1 MONTH OF FREE READING

at

www.ForgottenBooks.com

By purchasing this book you are eligible for one month membership to ForgottenBooks.com, giving you unlimited access to our entire collection of over 700,000 titles via our web site and mobile apps.

To claim your free month visit:

www.forgottenbooks.com/free50803

* Offer is valid for 45 days from date of purchase. Terms and conditions apply.

English
Français
Deutsche
Italiano
Español
Português

www.forgottenbooks.com

Mythology Photography **Fiction**
Fishing Christianity **Art** Cooking
Essays Buddhism Freemasonry
Medicine **Biology** Music **Ancient Egypt** Evolution Carpentry Physics
Dance Geology **Mathematics** Fitness
Shakespeare **Folklore** Yoga Marketing
Confidence Immortality Biographies
Poetry **Psychology** Witchcraft
Electronics Chemistry History **Law**
Accounting **Philosophy** Anthropology
Alchemy Drama Quantum Mechanics
Atheism Sexual Health **Ancient History**
Entrepreneurship Languages Sport
Paleontology Needlework Islam
Metaphysics Investment Archaeology
Parenting Statistics Criminology
Motivational

CHAPTERS

ON THE

SCIENCE OF LANGUAGE.

BY

PROF. LEON DELBOS.

WILLIAMS AND NORGATE,
14, HENRIETTA STREET, COVENT GARDEN, LONDON; AND
20, SOUTH FREDERICK STREET, EDINBURGH.

1878.

LONDON:
G. NORMAN AND SON, PRINTERS, 29, MAIDEN LANE,
COVENT GARDEN.

CONTENTS.

	PAGE.
PREFACE	iii

CHAPTER I.
ORIGIN AND FORMATION OF LANGUAGE . . . 1

CHAPTER II.
GRAMMAR 37

CHAPTER III.
ON THE LITERATURE OF INDIA 51

CHAPTER IV.
ETYMOLOGICAL VOCABULARY 71

CHAPTER V.
CLASSIFICATION OF LANGUAGE 104

PREFACE.

The task I have undertaken is not one without difficulties, but my subject is so full of interest, that I feel convinced it would be enticing, were it trusted in the hands of a still less skilful writer, for many will acknowledge with me, that few sciences, if any at all, can lay a more just claim to the attention of the thinking man than the Science of Language, since it treats of the greatest, most valuable and useful possession of mankind.

My object, in composing the present work, has been to condense into a small compass the results of former discussions on several interesting philological problems, chiefly for the benefit of those who have not had, either the leisure or opportunity of devoting their time to philology, and also with a view to induce some, who may never have read anything on the subject—either because they think it *dry*, or because they know not what mysteries the science of language will unfold—to begin a study which promises so rich a harvest.

Though the origin of language seems at first sight to be shrouded in almost impenetrable darkness, I have nevertheless attempted to give a solution of that interesting question, and if some should think it presumptuous on my part to write upon a theme which has been expounded before by such men as Grimm, Bopp, Burnouf, Max Müller, Renan, Farrar, and others of equal repute, I shall only remark that a man by far inferior to those eminent philologists, but who nevertheless has taken the trouble of studying his subject conscientiously, may have ideas which may not always be erroneous and worthless. And as this book is only a mere Introduction to a Science, far too important and extensive to be treated as fully as it ought to be, in a few pages, I hope those who will condescend to peruse this work, will not pass too severe a judgment upon its author.

LEON DELBOS.

London.

CHAPTERS ON THE SCIENCE OF LANGUAGE.

CHAPTER I.

ORIGIN AND FORMATION OF LANGUAGE.

It will not be out of place to take a survey of the several theories, which from time to time have been propounded by different writers, without, however, dwelling upon those which are mere fancies, and from which nothing, either important or useful, can be derived, such as the hypotheses of Lucretius, which can only be considered as the wild ideas of a poet totally under the influence of a fanciful imagination, and not as those of a philosopher who has acquainted himself thoroughly with his subject; or, again, those of the Brahmins, who imagined they had solved the problem of the origin of language, by attributing the invention of it to the goddess Sarasvati, wife of Brahma, to whom also they ascribed the invention of Sanskrit, that of music and of the letters called Devanagari; and, therefore, leaving these and the like unnoticed, we shall at once proceed to examine more rational conceptions.

The Grecian philosophers seem to have been the first who began the study of the subject in a scientific manner, as most of them have left MSS. treating of language; and although it must be acknowledged that their views have not always been erroneous, nevertheless their numerous and praiseworthy attempts have generally been fruitless and unsatisfactory.

After them the subject seems to have fallen into complete oblivion for many ages, for it was not until the middle of the last century that the question was brought forward again by some enthusiastic people, who pretended to have found the solution of the difficulty in the following two verses: "And out of the ground the Lord God formed every beast of the field, and every fowl of the air; and brought them unto Adam to see what he would call them: and whatsoever Adam called every living creature, that was the name thereof.

"And Adam gave names to all cattle, and to the fowl of the air, and to every beast of the field; but for Adam there was not an help meet for him."*

The thoughtful reader may be somewhat astonished when told that the above verses, far from throwing any light upon the origin of language, have, on the contrary, rendered it more dark than ever; for many have misinterpreted their meaning, and when they say that they contain the proof that language is of a divine origin, we cannot but admit that their understanding is so obliterated, that it makes them find in a text a meaning totally different from the one implied; for if we examine the two verses quoted and analyse them, nothing will be easier than to discover in them the proof that if God gave man the power of speech, God did not give him the words ready made, for it is said that Adam himself gave names

* Genesis, ch. ii., vers. 19, 20.

to all the beasts of the field and to every fowl of the air, and, therefore, by the text itself, we must acknowledge that the words were invented by man alone.

Others have said that Adam indeed named the different creatures brought before him, but that God had previously told him what names he was to use, and that thus the first man only repeated the words his Creator had taught him.

This last explanation has been admirably refuted by the eminent philologist Grimm : " If words have been created by God, says he, we must suppose that that communication was made to man before all others, for since God spoke to Adam it is necessary to believe that he was able to understand what the Creator was saying to him."

Moreover, from the same explanation it must be inferred that Adam was endowed with a prodigious memory, otherwise he would never have been able to recollect all the different words that were taught him in a few hours, and also that God took upon himself the task of teaching man very much in the same way as a master instructs his pupils in the knowledge of some dead or living language.

I am more inclined to believe that those who entertained such opinions were regardless of truth, and only anxious, as is unfortunately too often the case, to make the Scriptures suit their own views, or wished above all things and without reason to find in the above-quoted verses the canonical declaration of the divine origin of language. And thus they forgot that if God had been really the maker of language, language must have been perfect, or at least have been as much so as Latin, Greek or Sanskrit, for God is perfect and omniscient, and therefore the primitive idioms of mankind ought to have been as complete and elegant as those that followed them.

I am quite aware that some people who are never short of an answer, will boisterously declare that the primitive language itself was as rich in words as those we now speak, and that often without knowing any but their own tongue, and without thinking that the acknowledgment of such an idea is equivalent to affirm that a great many vocables and expressions used in our days were also used in remoter times for things which did not exist then, and unmindful or ignorant of the fact that man can only know the names of things which he has seen or heard people speak of.

It is here necessary to remark that thought and speech are intimately connected, and so much so, that if speech cannot exist without ideas, ideas in their turn cannot exist without speech; and if it be true to say that the intellectual and material parts of ourselves form a whole marvellously harmonized, although of very different essence, it will also be true to affirm that thought and the words which represent it are so closely united, that it is impossible to think without the words which represent the thought, occurring at once, and almost spontaneously to the mind.

This is so true that we cannot acquire a new idea without at the same time acquiring a new word in which the thought is enveloped; and that word itself is always generated at the very instant the thought is conceived.*

* The Greeks had so well understood this connexion between ideas and words, that λoyoς expressed not only the outward form by which the inward thought is expressed, but also the inward thought itself. Becker also says that "*Ideas without words are*

The great philosopher, John Locke, maintained that man lived for a considerable time in a complete state of dumbness, causing his thoughts—if thoughts can exist without words—to be known to his fellow-men by means of gestures and signs, and that he continued thus, until his ideas became so numerous, that he no longer found that *natural speech* sufficient, and then invented artificial means of communication which enabled him to converse and share his impressions with others.

Adam Smith and Dugald Stewart adopted almost the same theory, but they went further, and the former tried to prove that men, after having been speechless for ages, suddenly invented words, which were all verbs, whilst the latter maintained that nouns were the first utterances of man.*

---

without form and consequently are no ideas."—Organismus der Sprache, p. 6.

* I am inclined to think that the above-named philosophers have gone beyond reasonable limits, for it is impossible to determine with any degree of certainty, whether verbs have been first used or nouns, and moreover, it is not necessary to the solution of the problem under consideration.

At the same time it is interesting to think on the subject.

Verbs might have been used first, for we know that all roots are generally verbal. Verbs are also the essence of language, and by pointing out the object we speak of, we can do without expressing the name of it. It has been objected that the verb being the most complicated part of a language, it is not likely it should have been resorted to before a considerable time had elapsed, and also that in some languages of Eastern Asia the verb can hardly be said to exist, or at any rate it exists only in a rudimentary form. These seem strong arguments in favour of Stewart's theory, and yet if we consider that three tenses at most are necessary, we shall no longer be astonished at the fact that verbs in some languages are in a very imperfect state.

The greatest objection that can be raised against these different theories, which have been propounded by men who have known to win for themselves a place amongst the most celebrated philosophers of the world, is the organism of man; it is indeed impossible to conceive that man lived for a long time without any spoken language at all, unless we believe also that he, in his primitive state, had not the power of articulating sounds. But such a supposition leads us to think, and rightly too, that the primitive races of mankind were different from those that came later on, and that they had not the power of speech developed as fully as it is now, for it cannot be readily acknowledged that beings, created with all the organs necessary to the emission of sounds, could have been long in a state so little different from that of the brute, and also that God gave men an organ which was to be useless to so many of them.

What would then have been the object of the Creator in giving our first parents the power of speech, if it was to be of no use to them?

Could God have bestowed such a gift on his creature, a gift which was to distinguish man from the lower animals, and which will always be an insuperable obstacle in the way of those who compare themselves to beasts, and that creature remain for ages ignorant of such a divine favour?

I am aware that some philosophers in our time, building a theory upon the fact that a few animals have the power of imitating our gestures and voice, have been trying to persuade us that we descend from some monkey tribe, but as they have been forced to acknowledge that language is the great immovable stumbling-block (for as yet they have not carried their audacity so far as to wish us to believe that a well-taught parrot speaks as perfect a language as their own)—they have been compelled to have recourse to an invention which nothing can justify, namely, a *missing-link,* which if found would—at least so they say—demonstrate the truth of their statements. If their theory was to be received, and they hope it will at some future time, it would be, according to them, the proof that language has come through the other species of animals, undergoing changes, and constantly perfecting itself, until it received the last touch from man.

But the difference between the so-called language of a monkey and that of a human being is so great, that the former cannot be said to have any resemblance to the latter.

The cries of animals are due to instinct, and only correspond to a limited number of sensations; they are always the same, and they cannot be called words, because animals do not articulate.

But as few reasonable men entertain such ideas, I think the best thing is to leave those worthy philosophers to admire their own speculations, and since they seem to value greatly the honour of being the offspring of a chimpanzee, I do not see why we should unkindly try to snatch from their minds an idea which renders them proud and happy.

But to return to our subject, let us now examine what Grimm says concerning language.

According to that eminent philologist, language grows and develops itself in a special soil, exactly in the same manner as a plant or a tree, and he rejects the idea that man was created with a language.

"If languages," says he, "were an innate faculty of

man, a child of a given race, brought up in a foreign family, ought to speak the language of his parents." Grimm is right there, for this is never the case. I have myself known an English boy who had been educated among French people, and who came to England for the first time at the age of thirteen, unable to speak a word of his parents' language, while he could speak French as well as any child born in France of French parents.

He learnt English, rather slowly, and never was able to speak that tongue as an Englishman, and had that accent which is always the characteristic of a foreigner.

This simple fact shows the truth of Grimm's statement

"On the contrary," says the same grammarian again, "the language of animals never undergoes any change, and a dog reared in the midst of cats will bark like every other dog."

In short, we cannot compare the language of animals to that of man, and although we are aware that some people believe, or pretend to believe, that a dog is in possession of as polished and perfect a tongue as ours, yet if we reflect upon the fact that the way in which animals are reared has no influence whatever upon their cries or utterances, while, on the other hand, the language of man is transformed by different causes, we must come to the conclusion that sounds emitted by beasts are natural cries only.

Man also has a natural language which all men possess in common, and which is the same all over the surface of the globe. That tongue is made up of interjections and cries resembling those of the lower animals; but besides that we possess, and alone possess, the *artificial language*, which we must learn as every other branch of human learning, and which we never know until it has been taught us.

I know that M. Renan says that to invent language would have been as impossible as to invent a new faculty of the mind,* and that that eminent scholar further adds, that it is as absurd to call invention the use man made of speech to express his thoughts, as to call invention the use we make of our eyes to see, or of our ears to hear; and, moreover, he believes that language was created all at once and in its perfect state;† but if we read his book through, we shall further discover that the same writer states that were man to lose language he would invent it anew.‡

These statements are contradictory, and I must here confess, with all due respect to M. Renan, that I fail to understand what he means; for on the one hand he asserts that man cannot create language, and on the other he affirms that man has that power.

Now what conclusion can be drawn from the different opinions we have just examined? Are we to believe that God created language and gave it ready made to man? or that mankind, having been for a considerable time without speech, invented it? or again, that language was created by man alone, and successively? or that it was invented suddenly, and reached perfection at once?

We have given our reasons for not believing that God created man with a language or taught him one, and we have shown how impossible it is to admit that man was speechless for ages.

* "De l'Origine du Langage," p. 92.
† "De l'Origine du Langage," p. 16.
‡ "De l'Origine du Langage," p. 245.

To believe that language was created by man suddenly, and became perfect at once, is unreasonable; for perfection, in human nature, is always the fruit of time and study, though by *perfection* it must not be thought that I mean to imply that language is not susceptible of improvement. On the contrary, I acknowledge it is very imperfect, and that is another inducement for me to believe that it is not the creation of God; for I cannot conceive anything imperfect coming from the Creator of all things.

I think that language was not solely invented because it was a necessity for man to communicate his thoughts to his fellow-creatures, but also because, having received the divine gift of speech, he could not have been without one.

The faculty of creating words was in man, but if the words themselves are a human invention, the power of inventing them was a spark from the divine intellect, and it is in this sense that we may say that language truly had a divine origin.

In the beginning, and so long as man was alone, he did not speak; but as soon as a mate was given him, he felt the want of making her share his sensations in another way than by mere signs, and it was then that his mind, suddenly enlightened by a ray of the divine wisdom, revealed to him the gift he possessed in himself, and that for the first time words came forth from his mouth; words which must have been few, and which being repeated by woman became the foundation of the primitive language.

But they did not find themselves at once in possession of a fully-developed tongue. Every day brought under their eyes new objects, and other words, the representation of the sounds they produced were introduced, thus increasing daily the vocabulary of our first parents.

Their children naturally were taught their mother's tongue, and when they had become men and women, and began to work at different trades, they used fresh words and new expressions which still enriched the primitive vocabulary.

At the end of several generations, the offspring of the first man having spread over a considerable portion of the globe, the primitive language began to undergo changes. New things required new appellations, and the names of objects, plants, and animals which did not exist in their new country were forgotten. This shows that the change of country must have been the cause of great modifications in the maternal idiom of mankind, but it was not the only one.

As the number of men was daily increasing, and as their tastes are different, all those who had selected a particular kind of life collected together. Some who loved agriculture became pastoral nations; whilst others, preferring the dangers and pleasures of war to peace and quietness, became the roots of the warlike tribes which have at all times been only too numerous. It is not to be expected that the languages spoken by men of such different tastes should be alike. The pastoral nation had an idiom rich in words connected with agriculture, whilst that of the warlike tribe, deficient in such terms, had almost an innumerable quantity of words used to designate weapons or implements of war.

The difference of climate has also been one of the causes that have influenced language.

In the North, the mind, impressed by the sight of fields of snow, of seas of ice, of a thick atmosphere loaded with grey clouds, imparts the gloom of nature to the language, which is short, harsh, and unpoetical; whilst in the South, where everything invites man to enjoy life, and where Nature shows herself under the most pleasant aspect, the words are abundant, sweet and harmonious.

The Northern languages therefore are more suited to express gloomy and terrible ideas than the Southern ones, which are by far superior to the former, when it is desired to represent agreeable and voluptuous pictures.

Indeed the influence of the climate is so strong, that it modifies not only the language of a nation, but also the character of the people; and we all know that in Northern climes people are more phlegmatic and less passionate than in the South; that in their books they evince more coolness and correctness; that their reasoning is better, but their language not so elegant; in short, they are deeper and more philosophical than their Southern brethren.

In the sunny regions the reverse is the case. The brightness of the light seems to give a part of its brilliancy to the people, whose imagination, more brisk and sprightly, pictures things more vividly and boldly.

However, the language of Homer, Plato, and Aristotle —that king of languages through the medium of which some of the greatest treasures of ancient learning have been handed down to us—is a proof that there is no rule without exception.

At the same time it must be acknowledged that other influences besides those we have mentioned contributed to give the Greek language such a state of superiority over all the others, and it is here the place to mention the influence a government may have upon language.

In a country where—as used to be the case in Greece—men were at liberty to write their thoughts or to speak without hindrance or fear, the language becomes proud and clear; whilst, on the other hand, the tongue of a people oppressed by a tyrant is marked with the stamp of obscurity and respect; it is elegant, subtle, allegorical, and even mysterious, as is the case with some languages spoken in Eastern countries.

I think the reasons I have just enumerated prove that language, like everything human, changes, but nevertheless I shall not conclude this point without mentioning a few facts in support of the assertion.

Gabriel Sagard, who was sent as a missionary to the Hurons in 1626, and published his "Grand Voyage du pays des Hurons" at Paris in 1631, states that, among these North American tribes, hardly one speaks the same language as another; nay, that two families of the same tribe do not speak exactly the same language. And he adds, what is important, that their language is changing every day, and is already so much changed that the ancient Huron language is almost entirely different from the present one.*

We also read of missionaries in Central America who attempted to write down the language of savage tribes, and who compiled with great care a dictionary of all the words they could lay hold of. Returning to the same tribe after a lapse of ten years, they found that their dictionary had become antiquated and useless. Old words had sunk to the ground, and new ones had risen

* Quoted from Max Müller's "Science of Language."

to the surface; and to all outward appearance the language was completely changed.

Towards the end of the eighteenth century a colony of Normands crossed the ocean and settled on the coast of San Domingo, where they formed that tribe known under the name of "Buccaneers." After having been for twenty years without communication with the French, and although they had spoken their native language among themselves, it was hardly possible to understand them, so great was the difference between their new language and the former one.

The want of literary pursuit is a cause of the quick transformation of a language, and it has been remarked that the nations where the alphabet has not yet made its appearance are unable to retain the same language through several generations, for literature is there totally unknown, and as it is the only means by which a tongue can live, the idiom undergoes constant alterations which cannot fail to transform it into a new one in a very short time. It is only because language is written, and thus preserved in books, that its changes are so slow, but the language of nature is soon doomed to destruction.

The import of foreign words is another cause of the decay of language. So long as their number is small the change is scarcely noticeable. But if through some political event or other a nation is made to adopt a foreign language, a new idiom, closely related to those from which it shall have proceeded, but nevertheless perfectly distinct from them, will spring up.

For instance let us suppose the Greeks being made—through conquest or some other circumstance—to adopt the Italian language, or the Italians forced to use the

Greek tongue; they would each pronounce foreign words according to the sounds they give to their own letters, and retaining at the same time some of their own words, it would come to pass that in the course of time a great many new words would be introduced either in the Greek or the Italian, and would thus be the source whence a fresh idiom would spring; an idiom which after two or three generations would be an entirely new language, which would be as different from its parents as the Italian or Spanish are different from the Latin tongue from which they were both derived.

Among others, I shall choose Spanish as a living proof of the influence of conquest upon the idiom of a people.

The language of Spain was immediately derived from the Latin tongue, and for a considerable time was indeed nothing but Latin itself, until it had to undergo the changes to which all tongues are subject, thus forming a new idiom, but at the same time being still Latin. But when the Moors crossing the sea took possession of the southern part of Spain and became the lords and masters of the land, some of the words of their language crept slowly into the native idiom, and at last gave the Spanish language the stamp which distinguishes it from the other Romance dialects.

Yet in spite of the numerous Arabic words found in the language of Spain, Spanish is a Latin dialect, not that it came direct from the pure classical language of Italy, but it was derived from it through idioms of that tongue.

And if any one could entertain any doubt as to the right one has to call Spanish a modern Latin, a glance at the grammar of the language would soon cause all uncertainty to vanish.

Thus far I have been reasoning on the hypothesis that all languages have descended from one common speech. But as many persons reject this theory, it is necessary to say a few words in support of an opinion which is shared by the most eminent philologists and philosophers of our time.

If we at once admit that men have all sprung from one common stock, we can scarcely believe that they had several languages, when one only would answer the purpose, so long as the number of human beings remained small. We hold this a sufficient proof of the common origin of all tongues, and know that those who acknowledge the truth of the common origin of all men will side with us. But those who maintain that we have sprung from several different pairs will not so readily accept our way of reasoning; and although we should like to convince them, we cannot here undertake to prove that all men have had one father and one mother only; for this would be out of place in this essay, and besides the problem having so often been treated by the most eminent physiologists, we do not deem it worth our while to enlarge on a subject which, if studied carefully by a person who has gone to the trouble of weighing all the different opinions, will leave little doubt as to the origin of man.

But as Professor Max Müller very truly remarks, "the common origin of mankind is not a sufficient proof of the common origin of language, for language might have broken out at different times and in different countries among the scattered descendants of one original pair."*

* " Lectures on the Science of Language."

Those who support the theory of several primitive languages tell us that philologists have classified them into three different families, and that as no Monosyllabic, no Agglutinative languages have ever reached the Inflectional stage, it is necessary to admit that there must have been at least three primitive idioms: a Monosyllabic one, another Agglutinative, and a third one which has been the mould into which inflectional languages have been cast.

Unfortunately for the adversaries of the common origin of language, it happens that Professor Max Müller has proved that languages widely different from each other may have sprung from the same source.

I shall add that the three different grammatical forms exhibited in the three families of speech prove nothing against our theory, unless it may be proved that no Aryan language has ever belonged to the Agglutinative, or to the radical stages. Such a thing has never been proved, whilst on the other hand signs of Agglutination have been discovered in the Monosyllabic idioms, and that some Agglutinative dialects are becoming day by day nearer to the Inflectional stage.

Many have maintained that *no new language can be formed,* and that consequently all tongues now spoken must have existed ever since the time of the first appearance of man upon this globe, and they give this as a proof that several pairs of human beings were created at the same time, each with a different language.

If this were true, it would necessarily follow that two nations speaking different languages must be of different races; for instance, that the Germans and the English have come from different stocks. This needs no refutation.

The supporters of such ideas forget that they can go back to a time, not very remote, when their own mother tongue was totally unknown, and that every language now spoken gives birth to numerous dialects, which in their turn shall also become languages when their sources shall have become arid.

It has also been said that the number of idioms is decreasing, and that all languages now spoken seem to converge towards a certain point which as yet cannot be designated, and also that many dialects have become entirely annihilated.

Those supposed to be in that case are said to be the dialects of Greece, of Italy, and of France; and we are told that the more we look back the greater we find the number of dialects. This assertion is, I fear, erroneous; for if it be true that the more we penetrate into the realm of human speech the greater the varieties we find, it becomes at once a necessity to admit that the primitive human beings were in possession of a number of languages which puts into the shade the greatest linguists of the world, and compared to whom Mezzofanti himself was a beginner. I admit that many idioms and dialects have become a dead letter; but if I am told that the modern Greeks now speak one language only, that the Italians all use the "lingua Toscana," and that the peasants of Normandy or of the southern provinces of France speak the language of Voltaire, I shall be compelled to say in reply that such is not the case, and that at the present time there are numerous dialects of the languages above named. It must not also be forgotten that almost each class of society, each trade, each profession, has its own dialect. There is a language of the sailor, of the physician, of the soldier, of the scholar, of the sportsman; and such words as kevels, cleats, hod cephalous, splays, ramps, are words which do not belong to the common dialect.

Others say that as language is the representation of thoughts which are the same in every human brain, there ought to be one language only to express similar ideas, and they most erroneously conclude that languages have not come from the same source, an assertion which, by-the-by, would make us believe that the same thought cannot be expressed in different ways, and that, for instance, man, homo, homme, ἄνθρωπος, are different creatures, or that "How do you do? Wie befinden sie sich? Come sta? Como esta vd? Comment vous portez vous? hashalom lekâ?"* though expressed very differently, do not convey the same thought.

It must be borne in mind that the number of dialects is daily growing larger; that they spring forth from a tongue as the boughs from the main branches, and as the main branches sprang forth from the trunk; and since this takes place every day under our own eyes, what reason can there be to say that no new tongue can be formed when experience proves to the contrary?

See what Robert Moffatt, in his "Missionary Scenes and Labours in Southern Africa," says:—

"The purity and harmony of language," he writes, "is kept up by their pitches, or public meetings, by their festivals and ceremonies, as well as by their songs and

* הֲשָׁלוֹם לְךָ

their constant intercourse. With the isolated villagers of the desert it is far otherwise; they have no such meetings: they are compelled to traverse the wilds, often to a great distance from their native village. On such occasions fathers and mothers, and all who can bear a burden, often set out for weeks at a time, and leave their children to the care of two or three infirm old people. The infant progeny, some of whom are beginning to lisp, whilst others can just master a whole sentence, and those still further advanced, romping and playing together, the children of nature, through their live-long day, *become habituated to a language of their own.* The more voluble condescend to the less precocious; and thus from this infant Babel proceeds a dialect of a host of mongrel words and phrases, joined together without rule, and *in the course of one generation the entire character of the language is changed.*"

Another fact corroborates as strongly the truth of our statements namely, *that the words of almost every known tongue can be traced back to simple and unchangeable roots.*

These roots, which are monosyllables, can be used as words, and are indeed thus used in the Chinese and some other monosyllabic languages of a very primitive kind, languages in which there is scarcely any difference between nouns, adjectives, verbs, adverbs, and prepositions, everything being chiefly dependent upon the construction.* Or those roots may be joined together in such a manner that one of them modifies the sense of the other

* Webb de Burleigh. Essay on the probability that the language of the Empire of China is the primitive language. London, 1669.

to form a new word;* or again, two roots may both lose their independence in forming a new word;† but no new root has ever been added.

Three families of languages have thus been formed from one common source.

What that common source has been is what we cannot tell, nor any one else either, for the reason that the most ancient languages of which we have any notion, such as the Egyptian or the Chinese, are posterior by several thousand years, to the apparition of man on earth.

Some scholars, more enthusiastic than wise, have laid claims to the discovery of the primitive language, but the results of their labours have always been, as they were wont to be, fruitless.

Great has been the number of those who maintained that Hebrew had been the first language of mankind, simply because it was the one in which the Bible had been written. It is that belief which for a long time has prevented the science of language from making any progress, for a few idioms only could be traced back to Hebrew, whilst a quantity of others could not. Seeing this, some people began to ask themselves why Hebrew should have been the primitive tongue, and as no reason was found to support that assertion, and as, moreover, there is not a word either in the Ancient or New Testament in favour of it, the idea was at last abandoned; and it is from that time only, that the real era of discoveries in the linguistic science began to dawn; for when it was once acknowledged that the honour bestowed on Hebrew

* Turanian family of languages.
† Semitic languages.

rested on no sound basis, the enthusiastic scholars, above referred to, spared themselves no trouble to discover another tongue worthy of it, and in their enthusiasm almost every European language was in turn hailed as the progenitor of all the others, without any foundation or sense, as may be seen from a perusal of their works.

For instance, Goropius, in his book published at Antwerp in 1580, tried vainly to prove that Dutch had been spoken in Paradise. Andrew Kempe followed in the same groove, maintaining—very seriously too— that God spoke Swedish, that Adam answered Him in Danish, whilst the serpent addressed Eve in the French tongue. J. B. Erro published also a work,* in which he tells us that Basque† was the language of our first parents. A curious discussion also took place on the same subject about 200 years ago in the Metropolitan Chapter of Pampeluna, and the decision of the members entered in the minutes of the Chapter runs as follows :—

1. *Was Basque the primitive language of mankind?* The learned members confess that, in spite of their strong conviction on the subject, they dare not give an affirmative answer.

2. *Was Basque the only language spoken by Adam and Eve in Paradise?* On this point the Chapter declares that no doubt can exist in their minds and that "it is impossible to bring forward any serious or rational objection."

* "El mondo primitivo." Madrid, 1814.

† The Basque, called also euscára, escuára, or eusquéra, is the language spoken by the inhabitants of the valleys of the Spanish Pyrenees, near the angle formed by the western coast of France and the north of Spain.

It is not only in our time that such a vast amount of labour and real worth have been wasted, for we read that the ancients also tried to find out what language had been first in use, and as the experimental method seemed to them the most appropriate one, they resorted to it. Herodotus informs us* that Psametick, king of Egypt, wishing to know what language had been the primitive one, caused two new-born infants to be entrusted to the care of a shepherd, who was commanded never to speak to them, or even to let them hear the sound of a human voice. The two children were suckled by a she-goat, and no one ever approached them except the shepherd, who had been further told to watch them carefully in order to know what word they would first utter. After a time, it came to pass that the children pronounced the word Βέκκος. The king was at once informed of the fact, and the wise men of his country, on whom the task of finding the meaning of the word had devolved, discovered that it meant " bread" in the Phrygian tongue.

And probably because they were wise men, and without any further thought upon the subject, they came to the conclusion that Phrygian must necessarily have been the most ancient language, because it was the natural one, as they thought.

I am aware that some people, at present living, will share the opinion of the wise men of King Psametick, and I shall therefore say that both they and the wise men are wrong.

In the first place, it is not to be supposed that infants should at once ask for bread; it is more natural that they should ask for milk or pronounce those easy syllables of

* Herodotus, B. II. 2.

pa and *ma* as all the other infants do, and taking into consideration that those unfortunate creatures had known no other mother but a she-goat whose bleating was the only sound they ever heard, they simply imitated the voice of their nurse, and thus a mere interjection, a natural cry, was interpreted as a word. For though Βεκκος may have really meant bread in Phrygian, I do not hesitate to affirm that in this case it was a pure imitation of the bleating of the goat, and my assertion is further supported by the fact, that the Greeks often used to call a goat βῆκα.

After this, we cannot hesitate to say that the experimental method is utterly useless. And indeed, were it of any use, it ought to be condemned, for we have no right whatever to snatch away children from their mothers, for our own gratification, and I most sincerely hope that the time when such abominations could take place without rebuke is past for ever.

Some writers on philology think that, in the origin, language must have been complex instead of simple. But whether it is not more natural to believe that language grew up like everything else in Nature is what we will now examine? Nothing is likely to throw more light upon the subject than the way in which children learn their mother tongue.

They use only simple words which they connect without art, and have a tendency to employ all the verbs in the infinitive mood, and to make regular those which are not so, and nearly every one of us has heard children say "he comed," " he throwed me down and bursted my ball."

Mothers also tell us plainly that language has been originally very simple. When they teach their offspring their own tongue, they seem to become children again, they make their own language go back to its constitutive elements, they use short syllables, avoid long words or shorten them, and this we see every mother do, whatever her rank and position in life may be, and under any sky we please to wander. But so general a fact can only be the result of one of those laws of Nature herself, a law to which we must submit, because God has willed it.

This, and also an examination of the languages spoken by tribes where civilization has scarcely made its appearance, are convincing proofs of the simplicity of the primitive language. We know that many of those tribes make no difference between present, past, or future, that their vocabulary is very limited, and that they put the words in the order in which they occur to their mind without regard to grammatical relations. Sir Emerson Tennent in a letter to Sir John Bowring, governor of Hong Kong, writes: " The Veddahs are a race of harmless savages; who inhabit the forests in one of the eastern districts of Ceylon, between the mountains of Ouva and the sea. Their origin and history are unknown; but they are probably a remnant of the aborigines driven into their wilds many centuries ago by the Malabar invaders of the island, and from some unaccountable cause they have never returned to civilized life. They live by hunting, and are expert in the use of the bow. They lodge in caves, under the shelter of overhanging rocks, and frequently sleep in the trees out of the reach of the bears and other wild animals. Fruits, roots, and grain they consume when they can procure them; but they subsist chiefly on birds, fish, honey, and the products of the chase. They dry deer's flesh and carry it for barter to the confines of the inhabited country, whither some of the travelling Moors resort with clothes, axes, and arrow heads, to be exchanged for dried meat, ivory, and bees wax. In these transactions the wild Veddahs are rarely seen by the strangers; in the night they deposit what they have to offer in barter, and intimate, by established signals, the description of articles which they require in exchange, and which, being left the following evening at the appointed place, are carried away before sunrise.

"Their language contains some words so similar to the more ancient Singhalese that the civilized natives are enabled to communicate with them, though with difficulty; but Mr. Mercer, who held for some years an official appointment in the vicinity of their forests, told me that not only is the language of the Veddahs almost unintelligible to the Singhalese generally, but so imperfect in itself that much of their communication with each other is conveyed by signs, grimaces, and guttural sounds, which bear scarcely a resemblance to articulate words.

"This race are unable to count beyond the first four numerals. A Veddah who had been found guilty of murder, is now undergoing a long imprisonment in the gaol at Colombo, where he learnt to count his own fingers, but he has never been able to advance further, and seems bewildered by the unaccustomed idea of any numbers beyond.

"Mr. Atherton, the Government Agent at Batticaloa, was employed by the Government to induce these untamed creatures to become located in villages, and betake themselves to cultivating the ground; and he has to a great extent succeeded in several instances. He verified to me the statement of their incapacity to comprehend the smallest combination of numbers; and I remember, in illustration of this, that he mentioned to me an instance in which he had given twelve arrows to a Veddah to be divided between himself and two others; but so helpless was he that, after spreading them out on the ground, he failed in every attempt to reduce them to three equal portions."

This is another argument in favour of the theory of the simplicity of the primitive language, and those Veddahs above mentioned show us that language like everything human has grown and developed itself slowly and has only reached its present stage after having been perfected and increased by thousands of generations.

Now it remains for us to explain how language has been formed.

We have already said that the creation of woman was for man a complete revelation, and that he then discovered what power lay in him.

The first words used must have only been the names of objects or animals which could be seen, or felt, or smelled, or heard, or tasted, in short, the names of either creatures or things, which in some way or other produced a well-defined impression on one or more of the senses.

The power of imitation was called into exercise, and it is that power which has contributed in a great measure to the formation of the names of animals. Many of those names have come down to us almost unchanged. Thus we have the Sanskrit *kokila*, the Greek κοκκυξ, the Latin *cuculus*, the English *cuckoo*, the French *coucou*, which all recall to our mind the song of the bird so familiar to us.

We also have the Sanskrit *karava* from which are derived κοραξ, *corvus*, *crow*, *corbeau*. In Chinese most names of animals, as well as the names of things which produce a well-defined sound or noise, are imitations of that sound or noise.

"There is a law which runs through the whole of nature," says Max Müller in his admirable lectures on the "Science of Language," "that everything which is struck rings. Each substance has its peculiar ring. We can tell the more or less perfect structure of metals by their vibrations, by the answer which they give. Gold rings differently from tin, wood rings differently from stone; and different sounds are produced according to the nature of each percussion. It was the same with man, the most highly-organized of Nature's works. Man in his primitive and perfect state, was endowed not only, like the brute, with the power of expressing his sensations by interjections and his perceptions by onomatopoeia.

"He possessed likewise the faculty of giving more articulate expression to the rational conception of his mind. That faculty was not of his own making. It was an instinct, an instinct of the mind as irresistible as any other instinct."

I shall add that music, the primeval music, the natural one, such as the rustling of leaves agitated by the wind, or the roaring of the waves, gave birth to other words, and we have the proof that music has been an important factor in language in such words as *rustling, roaring, whistling, hissing, bleating,* and *mewing.* It is also worthy of notice that a constant relation between accentuation and music is known to exist in almost all languages, and more especially so in poetry.

I know that imitation could have been of no use in the formation of words which have no connection whatever with sound, and therefore the *onomatopoetic theory*, as well as the system of *interjections*, fail to explain the formation of the other words.

If man had not been able to utter words representing the ideas of things which can only be known through the light of reason; if he had only had a language purely onomatopoetic; then man would have been very little superior, in that respect at least, to the other animals.

But man was endowed with reason, he had the faculty of reasoning, of comparing, of weighing, of analysing, of appreciating and perceiving the qualities of objects, qualities which have been rendered by some combinations of sounds which were always the same, and which represented the ideas it was wished to express. Thus we see that words associated with the idea of pain, are harsh or grave; whilst those connected with pleasing sensations are soft and quick.

The names of the physical qualities of bodies follow the same law, and the words *heavy, thick, enormous,* compared with *light, thin,* and *small,* are an illustration of it. It is this association between ideas and sounds which alone has produced such expressive words as *Blitz* or Στρεφειν; the former, a beautiful representation of the rapidity of the lightning, and the latter, indicating, most vividly, the zigzag of the electric spark. We might also mention the Greek ψυλλος, a *jumper, Floh* in German a *flying-thing,* or *Loppe* in Danish a *runner,* all recalling to the mind the different attributes of the insect called a *flea.*

The names which express *ideas,* the *operations of the mind,* or other things totally immaterial have been formed by means of that great law, which I shall call the *law of Associations,* and such words as *soul, imagination, conception*, and hundreds of others are derived from objects to which they were supposed to have some kind of resemblance.

It was thus that roots were formed, and far from seeing in them the work of hazard, I discover in their creation the hand of the Almighty, by whom all things have been, are, and shall be.

These roots have been the constituent elements of all the tongues now spoken, and can be found in the words of most languages.

Their number is very limited, being about 500 or rather less. This is not a very extensive vocabulary, but however it is quite sufficient; for as we have said before, these roots can be joined together in different ways, and each root can give rise to about 50 derivatives, which at once gives us a vocabulary of 25,000 words.

There are few people indeed, if any at all, who know 25,000 words of one language, and many a peasant in England could be found whose stock of words is much below one thousand; whilst most well educated persons do not know more than four or five thousand words of their own mother tongue. Shakespeare, who of all writers known had the greatest command of language, wrote the whole of his plays with 15,000 words; and Milton composed his poetical works with 6000 only, whilst the Ancient Testament says all it has to say with 5642;[*] and Bunsen affirms that the language of the ancient sages of Egypt, consisted of about 1000.[†]

The Chinese language is made up of 450 monosyllabic roots. A different accentuation and combination of these

[*] Renan.—" Histoire des Langues Sémitiques," p. 138.
[†] "Egypt," pp. 453-491.

roots have formed the basis of the 80,000 words contained in the Chinese vocabulary.*

These derivatives have been formed from the roots either by the addition of one or more letters, or by the change introduced in the pronunciation of those roots.

It is to the discovery of Sanskrit, in the XVIIth century, that we are indebted for the knowledge of this fact, and it is also that ancient language which has enabled us to trace back nearly all the words of our modern tongues to those roots, and which has spread over the origin of language a light which ever since has guided the steps of the philologist in the right direction, and which prevents him from going astray, when engaged in solving many problems relating to language.

Roots exist in every language, but the syllables which have been added prevent one from recognizing them at once; and all the efforts that were made previous to the discovery of Sanskrit, were almost fruitless, for neither an English, nor a French, nor a German word could be traced farther back than Latin or Greek; and the Greek word, which often was as complicated as the one to which it had given birth, remained a mystery because the old language of India was unknown to us.

Thus the English *Father*, the German *Vater*, the Gothic *Fadar*, the French *père*, the Italian and Spanish *Padre*, the Latin *pater*, could all be easily derived from the

---

* This fact, and the want of grammatical forms have caused the language of the empire of China to be considered as the primitive language of mankind, or at least as one of the oldest.

See Webb. de Burleigh.—" Essay on the probability that the language of the Empire of China is the primitive language.'' London, 1669.

Greek πατηρ; but nothing more, whilst the Greek in its turn can now be derived from the Sanskrit noun *Pitri*, which noun in its turn comes from the simple root *pâ*, which means *to nourish*.

In the same manner we shall find that the root *mâ*, meaning *to bring forth*, has produced the Sanskrit *mâtri*, the Greek Μητηρ, the Latin *mater*, the French *mère*, the Italian and Spanish *madre*, the German *mutter*, the English *mother*, the Russian *mat*, and perhaps also the Chinese *mou*.

Names expressing the different degrees of relationship are not the only ones whose etymologies can thus be ascertained. For instance, from the Sanskrit *man*, to think, we can easily derive the Greek μενω, the Latin *meno*, the Gothic *man*, the German *meine*, the English *mean*; and from the same root was formed the Sanskrit *manas*, whence the Greek μενος, the Latin *mens*, the Gothic *munds*, the German *meinung*, the English *mind*, the Russian *mnienie*, and also the English word *man*, which thus means *a thinking being*, and we can assign to the same etymology to the German *mann*, the Gothic *mann*, and the Russian *muz*.

But, as it is not my object to give etymologies in this place, and as I only wish to show how words were formed from roots, I shall only give one more example of derivations, the first ten numbers in fourteen different languages, and shall refer the reader to the Etymological Vocabulary contained in the present work.

A glance at the following table will show, very clearly, the relations which exist between the numbers of the languages we have chosen; and the reader will easily perceive that the differences between the numbers of one

ORIGIN AND FORMATION OF LANGUAGE. 33

tongue and those of another, consist chiefly in the change of the letters; and he is sure also to notice that those differences are very slight. For instance, we find that the initial letter in all the words for the number 2 are d, t, and z; but t and z belong to the same class of sounds as d; they are all dental letters, and such a change of letters is one of those determined by Grimm's law.

Again, in the number 3, we find as the initial letter the dental *t*, which only once is replaced by a *d*, and in the numbers 6 and 7 we find the sibilant, except in Greek.

Numbers.	1	2	3	4	5	6	7	8	9	
Sanskrit	aika	dvi	tri	chatur	pancha	shash	saptan	ashtan	navan	dasha
Zend	aeva	dva	thri	chatvar	panchan	chsvas	saptan	astan	navan	dasha
Greek	εις	δυο	τρεις	τεσσαρες	πεντε	ἑξ	ἑπτα	ὀκτω	ἐννεα	δεκα
Latin	unus	duo	tres	quatuor	quinque	sex	septem	octo	novem	decem
Italian	uno	due	tre	quattro	cinque	sei	sette	otto	nove	dieci
Spanish	uno	dos	tres	cuatro	cinco	seis	siete	ocho	nueve	diez
French	un	deux	trois	quatre	cinq	six	sept	huit	neuf	dix
Gothic	ains	twai	threis	fidwor	fimf	saihs	sibun	ahtau	niun	taihur
German	eins	zwei	drei	vier	fünf	sechs	sieben	acht	neun	zehn
English	one	two	three	four	five	six	seven	eight	nine	ten
Icelandic	einn	tvau	thryú	flogur	fimm	sex	sjau	atta	niū	tiu
Gaelic	aon	da	tri	ceithar	coig	sia	seachd	ochd	noi	deich
Russian	odin	dwa	tri	chetyre	piat	shest	sem'	osm	dewyat	desya
Lithuanian	wienas	dvi	trys	keturi	penki	sheshi	septyni	ashtuni	dewyni	deshi

Now, the above table will also illustrate the law which has presided at the formation of roots, viz., the law of Associations; for we can reduce the number 1 to the root *ûn*,* which means *to isolate*; the number 2 to the

---

* The number 1 may also be derived from the Sanskrit pronoun *aikas*, which means *alone*. *Aeva*, in Zend, from *aïva*, that. The feminine μια comes evidently from the adverb μειον less, in Sanskrit *mīnas, taken from.*

root *dau, to cut equally;* whilst we can derive 3 from *tar, to intercalate;* 4, from *chat, to divide;* 5, from *pach, to clench the fingers,* probably from the habit of counting on the fingers; 6, from *saj, to join;* 7, from *sād, to fill,* or from *saj, to adhere;* 8, from *ach, to spread,* or *aks* to occupy; 9, from the adjective *nava, new,* as being the last number; and 10 from *das, to cut off,* probably on account of its being the end of the series.*

The above few derivations are sufficient to show how great is the importance of Sanskrit to the philologist, since it enables him to trace words back to a language which is much nearer the primitive tongue than either Greek or Latin.

Though so old a language, Sanskrit is the most perfect and logical idiom that can be imagined, and as the language of a people is more or less the reflection of the civilization it enjoys, it follows that the Aryas were a highly polished race, at least three or four thousand years ago.

The eight cases of the Sanskrit, its three genders and numbers, its conjugation, so clear and so harmonious, can stand the comparison with the Greek tongue.

And if it be true that the simplicity of Arithmetical terms is an evidence of the advancement of the science of a nation, it will be necessary for us to come to the conclusion that the Hindoos of old were not only grammarians, but also arithmeticians.

Every one knows that most nations of the globe have

* The numbers 6 and 7 are found in languages of very different families, such as the Arabic and Hebrew and the Basque. In Arabic they are settah and sabah; in Hebrew, shēch and sheba; and in Basque, sei and zarpi.

always made use of a decimal system of notation, a system which has been derived from Nature and from the practice of counting on the fingers. When this decimal arithmetic is not found, we are almost certain to find in its place a quinary or vicenary scale, both of which are also derived from Nature, viz., the five fingers of one hand or the ten fingers and ten toes.

If we examine the numerals of the Indo-European family, we shall see that they are formed very regularly from one to ten, and that from ten to twenty the general method has been to add, to the ten simple numbers, the word ten; but some languages have departed from that simple rule.

In the Germanic idioms, for instance, the numbers *eleven* and *twelve* are not formed regularly; but in the Sanskrit we find for 11, 12, 13, 14, 15, 16, 17, 18, 19 the words *aikadashan, dvadashan, tridashan, chaturdashan, panchadashan,* up to nineteen, which is generally formed like the Latin *unus de viginti*, and is *unavinsati*.

From 20, in Sanskrit, *vinsati* for *dvinsati*, the other tenths are formed regularly by multiplying ten by the first ten numbers.

Simple and beautiful as this rule is, it has been broken through by a nation whose language is almost universally learnt, viz., by the French, who, instead of the simple words *septante, octante,* and *nonante,* make use of the complicated expressions *soixante-dix, quatre-vingt,* and *quatre-vingt-dix,* and who, instead of *ninety-six,* say *quatre-vingt-seize* (four twenties and sixteen).

I must also add that the figures we use, and which we are in the habit of calling Arabian numerals, have only been introduced into Europe by the Arabs, who had themselves learnt them from the Aryas.

And now that we have briefly shown how language may have sprung from one common source, and in what manner we are to understand that tongues have had a divine origin, we shall say a few words about an invention which has been the necessary consequence of that of language, and of the progress of the human mind, viz. Grammar.

CHAPTER II.

Grammar.

"Unter allen Völkern der Erde ist die Grammatick beinahe auf einerlei Art gebaut." — Herder: "Ueber die Ursprung der Sprache," p. 222.

Grammar, contrary to the opinion entertained by most people, and in spite of the apparent dissimilarity of its forms in different languages, is however neither the result of hazard nor of fancy, but is the natural want of the mind, and the consequence of the progress of man's intellect. Language, without Grammar, could never have reached the degree of perfection it has now attained—nay, it could scarcely ever have been of any use to mankind, for it is of the utmost importance that the words should be placed in a certain logical order, that they may show the first elements in which every thought can be decomposed. And the laws and rules which govern and bind those elements together, always correspond to the intellectual operations of the mind, by which ideas are co-ordinated and combined together.

Therefore, the rules of Grammar have not been created for the sake of rendering language more intricate, but on the contrary to make it more clear and more intelligible; they have been guessed by the mind, and psychologic analysis alone can enable us to understand their usefulness and necessity.

Our first conceptions are always connected with the different objects surrounding us, objects which never fail to make some impression or other upon one or more of our senses, and which enable us to form some idea of their primary quality, which is that of *substance*.

The mind, having acquired the notion of that quality, is led to designate all the different objects which are scattered upon the surface of the earth, or which surround us, and the words thus employed have been most wisely called *substantives* by all grammarians, who, in that respect seem to have only obeyed a sort of intuition of which they were not conscious.

After words had been used in a general sense, it became evident that a distinction between the different kinds or species ought to be made, and genders were then introduced.

It must also have been a general tendency to repeat the word twice, in order to give more force to the expression, as is indeed the case in Hebrew; but that reduplication, in the course of time, became a source of confusion through the ever increasing number of homonyms, which would soon have rendered language unintelligible, had not the signification of such words been fixed by the name of the species being made to precede that of the kind, as is exemplified by some of the words of our modern tongues.

But substantives alone are only the representation of simple and independent ideas, without any other quality but that of substance; and as this quality is only one out of many which must necessarily be expressed, another class of words which fulfils this object, has been invented and designated by the appellation of *Adjective*.

And although in several languages, one might be inclined to consider the substantive and adjective as the same class of words, it must be borne in mind that it is impossible to assimilate matter with its properties, and though it is perfectly true to say that adjectives are often derived from nouns, and that sometimes the quality expressed by the adjective is ascribed to the noun, yet it fails to prove that the attribute of the substance and the substance itself are the same thing.*

With nouns and adjectives, it was already possible to designate the different objects together with their several attributes; but those objects, besides names and qualities, move or are moved, act or are acted upon; in short, they exist, they *are,* and the part of speech under the head of which these important words are placed is the *Verb,* which therefore serves to express the different states of existence, and which the Chinese very appropriately call *Ho-tsen,* or the *living word.* The verb must and does always contain the idea of existence, and as it expresses that something *is,* or that an action is performed, there must necessarily be something being or acting, and it is the agent which has been called the *subject.* This subject can occupy three different positions in speech. It is the one who speaks, or the one to whom one speaks, or the one spoken of. These three modifications have been designated by the name of *Persons.*

* If this assimilation is grounded upon the fact that some adjectives are derived from nouns, it will be quite as reasonable to maintain that they can be assimilated to verbs, for many adjectives expressing activity or action are derived from verbs.

But when an action is done, there must of course be some one or something on which it is effected, that is to say, an *object,* called sometimes *accusative* or *regimen.* It is here necessary to remark that from the above definitions it is clear that nothing but a verb can bind the subject to the object, and that consequently every sentence must contain at least one verb.

But it is not sufficient to emit isolated words or sentences, for our intellect perceives between ideas and thoughts certain relations which must be expressed by some particular kind of words, in order that the development of our ideas may not be wanting in precision and quickness.

The relations that are found to exist in the intellect are of two kinds only, namely, the relation we perceive between two elements of the same thought, and the one we establish between two complete thoughts. *Prepositions* denote the first kind of connection, whilst the words used to join together two thoughts are called *Conjunctions.* These words do not in reality belong to the thought itself, and they must only be considered as the outward form of it, that is to say they are only *words.*

It has been deemed necessary to add some other classes of words to the preceding ones, in order to render the expression still clearer, more elegant or complete, and thus *articles, numeral adjectives, demonstrative pronouns,* have been introduced. These are so closely related to nouns, that they ought not to be considered as distinct classes of words; and especially so, when it is borne in mind that they do not really represent ideas different from each other. If some languages are compared together, it will be found that a demonstrative pronoun in any one particular tongue may become an article in another one: this would never occur were they the phonetic types of two ideas.*

Every one knows that the article is not positively necessary. Latin was deprived of it as also was Sanskrit, and in these two languages the deficiency thus existing was sometimes supplied by using pronouns, and the Greek article itself, instead of really determining the sense of words, is rather the expression of divers grammatical relations, as is proved by the modern Greek, in which it has been thought necessary to introduce fresh articles, and also by Apollonius in his "Syntax."†

The actions expressed by verbs may have taken place in different manners, or at different times, and as the expression of these modifications are of the utmost importance to the clearness of speech, words of another class have been resorted to. These words have no connection with each other, and as they always, or nearly always, are placed near the verb whose sense they modify, they have been called *Adverbs*. Some of these are nothing but prepositions, and others are joined to substantives when they are taken in a general or metaphorical sense; but they never modify nouns, because the nature of these would then be completely altered.

Adverbs are only affixed to adjectives, or verbs, or other adverbs; and in all languages known they are invariable.

* The so-called indefinite article is generally the numeral adjective *one*. The English language is an exception.

† Ἐστιν ἴδιον ἄρθρων ἡ ἀναφορά, ἡ ἐστι προκατειλεγμενου προσωπου παραστατικη.

Apollonius. "De Syntaxi," p. 31. Sylburg edition.

Relative pronouns are mere conjunctions, for they generally bind two parts of a sentence, and are in nowise a particular class of words; and the variations which they sustain in some languages do not in the least change their conjunctive property.

Personal pronouns have no more claims to form a separate class of words than the former ones, for although they are general enough to apply to all persons, yet they are nothing but nouns, being as well defined and as susceptible of modifications as those, as is proved by some languages in which they are declined exactly as substantives.* Moreover they do not always take the place of nouns, for in the Maya and some other idioms, they are used instead of the substantive verb, and in the Semitic languages and other African and American tongues, they take the place of the auxiliaries.

Everything seems to indicate that personal pronouns have very likely been formed first,[†] for man's first impression is that of his own existence, and I think it is more natural for us to attribute to all things an existence similar to our own, than to conceive them not endowed with any living principle. This being the case, how could we admit, with many grammarians, that the pronoun of the third person did not originally express a real person.

It was the idea of activity which is inherent in the verb, which has compelled grammarians to personify things, whose existence was expressed by that pronoun

* In Persian and Finnic.

† This opinion has been first propounded by the illustrious G. de Humboldt in his memoir, "Ueber die Verwandischaft der Ortadverbien mit dem Pronomen in einigen sprachen."

and thence the pronoun thus used has been thought to have changed its nature. Some languages possess a pronoun for inanimate things, but far from being always used for what it was intended, it is also used in speaking of living creatures as is shown by the English language, in which *it* can be used for the names of animals.

It was also the personification above referred to, which introduced the *genders*.

These genders were generally determined by nature herself, and remained a natural division, until they became, what they now are in most languages, namely, only a *grammatical necessity*, that is to say they were henceforth determined chiefly by the endings of the words. Thus, we see that the terminations of masculine nouns are more strongly accented than those of feminine ones, whilst some intermediate sounds were classified as *neuter* ones.

Numbers were also taken into consideration and new inflections were invented, to distinguish between *singular* and *plural*, and in some languages, when two objects only were spoken of, a difference was made introducing new endings. The formation of numbers in different languages is most irregular, for instance, in Hebrew things that can be counted can, when over ten, be put either in the singular or the plural.

Sometimes also, as in Chinese, many words have no plural at all, and the numbers are determined by the genders;* in other languages different forms are resorted to, and the plurals of inanimate things are different from those of animate ones.†

* The names of inanimate things have no plural in Chinese.
† In Persian and a few other tongues.

The *dual* is used in Hebrew and Keltic, but only for things which are naturally double, such as *the hands, the feet, the eyes*, and in Sanskrit, Greek, and most Slavonic tongues, it is used only in speaking of things accidentally coupled together.

Other wants have necessitated other inflections, for the signification of a word does in nowise depend upon the place of the other, or their order in the sentence, and as it was indispensable to mark the accidental relations which thought establishes between nouns, other inflections were introduced and added to the stem of the word, which itself was never altered.

These modifications which have received the name of *cases* constitute the *declension*.

In the most imperfect languages, every kind of relation was expressed by a different case and we have the Basque with eighteen cases; the Lapland with fourteen; the Armenian with ten; the Sanskrit and Slavonic with eight: the old German with six; the Greek with five; the Arabic with three only in the singular and two in the dual, whilst they have been totally eradicated from the Romance languages and the Vulgar Arabic, in which prepositions are used in their stead.

A quantity of cases is not at all necessary, for there can only be three kinds of relationship between words, viz., substance and accident (genitive case); cause and effect (dative and ablative), and union or community (accusative).

In most languages, adjectives which expressed only an absolute idea have remained unchanged, whilst in others, for the sake of grammar, they took inflections similar to those of nouns, and were always made to have the same number, gender, and case as the nouns they qualified; and as the attributes of substantives do not always express the same idea, and as they can be viewed under different aspects, modifications expressing these differences have become necessary, and thus while the *positive*, which affirms the quality, was the adjective in its original form, the *comparative*, which compares between two things, and the *superlative*, which is properly speaking the comparison between more than two nouns, received different forms by means of suffixes which distinguished them from each other and both from the positive.*

These degrees of comparison were at first formed by the adjunction of adverbs to the positive as in Basque,† or by the reduplication of the adjective itself, until finally the different degrees of comparison were marked by endings proper to each of them.

The verb was of all the different classes of words the one whose stem received the greatest number of changes. Inflections were used to denote the *tenses*, others to point out the persons. In some idioms, the personal pronouns were added to the verb, whilst in others they were not used along with it, and we also see that in some tongues, verbs were also modified according to the gender of the subject governing the verb.

* According to Benloew, the Comparative and Superlative degrees may be considered as the declension of the adjective. He assimilates the comparative to a dual and the superlative to a plural.—" De l'Accentation dans les langues Indo Européennes," p. 251.

† In Basque, the comparative is formed by adding *ágo* or the adverb *baño*, and the superlative by means of adverbs added to the positive and which correspond to the English *very*. These adverbs are *chit, chittez, gurtiz, guciz,* and *anitz*.

This last distinction was a very unnecessary one, and only a complication, for the verb can only express an absolute form of existence, and whether the subject be masculine or feminine is of no consequence, for it cannot have any effect upon the signification of the verb.*

Although there are inflections which are used to point out that an action has taken place, yet it would be a mistake to think that such modifications were a necessity, for they seem to have been chiefly grammatical differences, and this assertion is corroborated by the grammar of some ancient and modern tongues. We know that the future is used instead of the present in the Arabic; that the present in Hebrew does not really exist, and is expressed by the preterite or future. It may seem strange that a language should have no present tense, and yet if we only think a little, it will be easy to see that such a tense is not necessary, nay, that such a tense does not really exist, for the present expresses that the action has just been accomplished, but when it is expressed it must have already taken place, and consequently it is past.

In other languages, it is the future which is wanted, and its deficiency is supplied by auxiliaries joined to the infinitive, as is the case in English, in German, and some idioms belonging to the North American family.

The modern Greek also has lost the future, which is substituted by the present, preceded by the particle θa, or by prefixing the verb $\theta \epsilon \lambda \omega$, *I will*, to the aorist.

The tenses themselves are subordinate to different actions. Sometimes, as in the indicative and imperative, the action remains absolute, or it may, as in the condi-

* The third person has genders in the Slavonic languages, whilst in Arabic it is the second, and in Hebrew the first.

tional or subjunctive, be dependent upon another one, and is then possible or necessary, and these differences of meaning which constitute the *moods,* have also their peculiar inflections.

The simplest mood is the *Infinitive,** for it points out the action or existence vaguely and without any respect to person or number, and can therefore have neither gender, nor case, nor number.

Infinitives have been, and are even now, used as nouns in some languages, among which are the Basque, the Chinese, and the Greek; but in the latter language, in which they were called προαιρετικα ρηματα, they were indeclinable and had no genders.

Participles, instead of being as verbs, constructed with a subject, are constantly connected with nouns, whose meanings they always modify, and they can therefore be assimilated to adjectives, although participating of the nature of verbs, because they are always derived from them, and because also they express a different form of existence.

The different actions expressed by verbs, are not always of the same kind, for the subject may be acting upon something, or be acted upon or act upon itself, and thence three different ways of conjugating have sprung. The first has been called the *Active voice,* the second *the Passive,* and the third *Reflective* or *Middle.*

Besides these logical distinctions, some languages exhibit numerous others, such as *affirmative* and *negative* conjugations, or conjugations used for *persons* and others for *things,* or again, as in the Sanskrit, different forms

* In Arabic, as well as in some other languages, there is no infinitive.

serve to distinguish between the action profitable to the subject, and that hurtful to the same agent.

Scarcely any doubt can be entertained as to these distinctions being pointed out by means of auxiliaries, which in the course of time became incorporated with the verb itself; and judging by the analogies existing between most modern tongues and those languages of old, we have every reason to believe that the verb *to be* must have always been the most important auxiliary, though several others must necessarily have been in use, as well as some words which were not verbs, and among which personal pronouns occupy the chief place, and we know that, in Hebrew, as well as in some other Oriental languages, these pronouns denote a future tense, when they are placed before the verb, but a past, if they follow it.

We cannot say anything concerning the syntax peculiar to every tongue, because the laws which govern the order in which words succeed each other, are not fixed by necessities inherent in the intellect.

Syntax constitutes a difference between two languages, and sometimes between two nations, for men do not differ because they were born in different parts of the globe, but because their intelligence and ideas are not the same.

The more the syntax follows the logical order, the more polished the nation where it is in use, and the more developed the minds of its inhabitants must be. On the other hand, a primitive and ignorant race of men have a tendency to overthrow that logical order, which constitutes the superiority of one language over another.

There is certainly no language in which a perfectly logical construction exists, but at the same time the most polished idioms seem to come nearer to it day by day, as is proved by the tendency we now have to drop some antiquated constructions which can only hinder the progress of language and render it more obscure, thereby preventing its spreading over a larger portion of the globe.

Whether at some future time a perfectly logical syntax will be found to exist in a language, is what no one can determine at present; but we do not hesitate to affirm, that if the human intellect progresses enough to achieve such a conquest, the world shall then soon be in possession of a *universal language*.

But until the mind of man shall have attained to such a high degree of perfection, the nations of the earth will continue to use their own dialects, which will only be liable to the transformations that are the necessary consequences of the causes we have enumerated in the first part of this work.

It is here the case to remark that those who have entertained the idea of inventing a universal language, were, either ignorant of the laws which govern it, or were so blind as not to see the madness of their own design, and we shall always regret to see the names of some of the greatest men of Europe associated with such an unreasonable conception.

It is our duty to work indefatigably for the enlightenment of all, but we should never attempt to realize things which are far beyond the power of mortal man, for by so doing we lose a time, which if applied to the right thing would bear fruits, and certainly benefit mankind at large.

It is by work only, and by persevering inquiry into all

the different branches of Science, and not by mere speculation, that we may hope some day to see Truth victorious, and that no longer hampered by the fetters of ignorance and superstition, blind credulity destroyed for ever, will make room for Knowledge and Reason; and that man shall then have a right, and a lawful claim, to consider himself as the *chef-d'œuvre* of Nature.

CHAPTER III.

On the Literature of India.

When two hundred years ago, or thereabout, it became known that there was in India a language, which though spoken at the time of King Solomon, and though older by many centuries than the oldest languages of Europe, was not yet dead, but, on the contrary, was used by the Brahmins in preference to the modern tongues of India, the curiosity of the European scholars was so aroused, that several set out for India, where, after endless difficulties and toils, they succeeded in mastering the language of the Vedas.

It was only after they brought the results of their efforts to Europe, that the science of language, which till then, left unguided, had wandered here and there without effecting any valuable discoveries, and freed from the bonds which had so long impeded its progress, burst upon the world, which it astonished, and though the youngest among Sciences, soon became one of the most important.

A language which had brought about such a revolution was sure to secure the attention of the scholar and philosopher alike, and it has, indeed, ever since been studied most carefully, though not so generally as might be desired, by both.

We have seen, in a previous chapter, that Sanskrit taught us that most European languages were its offspring, but valuable as this is, it has revealed to us things of far greater importance, for they no longer interest the scholar alone but mankind at large, and more especially so the large Indo-European family, whose origins are so intimately connected with those of the Aryas of India, that they cannot now be separated.

If any one had been bold enough, a hundred years ago, to say that Europe, with its sciences, its arts and literature, was indebted to India for these benefits, and that this very civilization, of which we are so proud, was only the continuation of a civilization equally advanced, but flourishing three thousand years ago at least, many would have laughed but few would have believed. And if besides it had been pointed out that those affinities between India and Europe were not confined to sciences and arts, but that they existed more or less in the different forms of government, and in the various religions of both countries, people would not have hesitated to condemn the propounder of such doctrines as a visionary, though these assertions, as we shall see, were facts which are now acknowledged by every one who has made a conscientious study of the subject.

This change is also the work of Sanskrit and its literature. The first scholars who succeeded in gaining an insight into the literature of India, endeavoured, and succeeded in bringing parts of it to Europe, and as they have had numerous imitators we are now in possession of the greater part of the books of the ancient Hindoos, books which we can now study at home without going to the trouble of performing a voyage to India.

What vast amount of knowledge has been derived from this old Indian literature is what cannot be fully told in a work of this kind, for to do it justice would be to increase the bulk of this book beyond the intended limits, and therefore, we shall confine ourselves to a few pages, in which we shall give a short analysis of the chief works of Indian literature, merely noticing their chief points of interest, as well as the religious symbolism they exhibit, leaving the more minute examination of what they contain, to the future and another work.

The "Rig-Veda" is by far the most important portion of Sanskrit literature, for being the most ancient it is the one in which we may reasonably expect to look for a greater amount of information respecting India, its religion and civilization.

The "Rig-Veda," or book of the hymns, contains upwards of a thousand hymns, the beauty and simplicity of which cannot but strike, for the Arya, to judge him after the language of the "Rig," must have been the most candid and frank of men. He asks of his gods to give him riches, to pour down upon him all kinds of gifts and favours, and is no less eager in the requests he makes for the utter annihilation of those whom he considers his enemies.

The Arya had not yet learned to pray for his adversaries, and it was reserved for a higher philosophy to make men do what is most repulsive to their untutored nature.

We can also gather from the "Rig" what were the habits and occupations of the primitive Aryas.

All the prayers, all the supplications of the "Rig" are addressed to the two gods they most were in need of, namely *Agni* and *Indra*, and it would seem that the whole of the Aryan worship was centred in these two deities, the former the *Sun* and the latter, worshipped chiefly by the warriors, the *Ether*.

It is indeed natural, that men who had to encounter formidable enemies, each day opposing their advance, should have striven, by all means in their power, to secure the favours of so powerful an auxiliary as the mighty *Indra*, just as the European soldiers used to invoke the god of battles before attacking the foe, and that when once they had succeeded in acquiring the land they had coveted, they should invoke with no less ardour the God who alone could ripen their harvest—the *Benevolent Agni*.

The *Rig* opens and closes with a hymn to *Agni* the God of Fire (*Ignis*), whom the poet also calls *Angiras* (*the burning*), *Rita* (*the pure, the shining, the light*), *Surya*, the "*resplendent*" (from *Sur*, to *shine*), *Savitri*, the Creator (from *Su*, to *produce*), *Mitra*, the "*benevolent*" (from *Mid*, to *conciliate*), *Bhaga*, the "*fortunate*" (from *Bhay*, to *honour*). Then come invocations to *Vayu*, the *Air*; to *Indra*, the *Ether*, or rather the Heavens which encompass the Earth, to *Mitra* and *Varuna*, the *Sun* and the *Waters*; to the *Asvins* or morning and evening twilights; to *Sarasvati*, the goddess of speech; and to the *Ritus* or *Seasons*. We also find in the "Rig-Veda" hymns to divers inferior deities, among which may be mentioned those addressed to the *Ribhus*, that is to say to the *souls of the departed*.

Varuna, we are told in one of the hymns, is the *Son of Aditi*. This *Aditi* (a word evidently formed from *diti*, *divisible*, and *a* privative), means the "*indivisible nature,"* which is thus personified and whose sons, the *Adityas,* are constantly at war to repel the incessant attacks of the *Dityas* or *Evil spirits.*

The *Winds* are also addressed as the *Marus,* whose terrible chief *Rudra* (from *Ru,* to *run,* to *rush*), seems to be only a personification of the air, and another name for *Vayu.*

Soma, the Moon; *Usha,* the dawn (from *ush,* to shine); *Vishnu,* the three steps of whom are a symbol of the Sun at morn, at noon, and at eve, and whose ninety-four stations are the sum of numbers representing divers astronomical phenomena, have all their worship as well as the *Venas* or *clouds.*

From the above, we gather that the worship of the primitive Aryas, like that of almost every nation in its infancy, has had its origin in the contemplation of the marvels which surround us, and of the phenomena which are calculated to impress strongly the minds of men. These phenomena are of two kinds, beneficial and hurtful. The first ones have been ascribed, by men ignorant of the chief laws which govern Nature, to some benevolent divine being, whilst the latter have been considered as the work of the evil spirits.

Thence arose this ancient belief in two antagonistic principles, the one *good* the other *evil.*

The darkness of night, superseding the brightness of day, cannot but have strongly impressed the minds of those who first beheld it. The night has been looked upon as the enemy of the day; the former has become the *evil principle,* and the latter the *good one,* and men have worshipped both, the *evil one* to pacify him, to prevent him from harming them, and the *good one* in grateful acknowledgment of his favours and also to implore him to continue them.

Such a worship may seem very low to those who never go to the trouble of thinking, but to the philosopher, it exhibits more true philosophy, and more reason, than one might at first suppose.

This glorious luminary, source of heat and light, may well be regarded as the giver of all good things, and of all things necessary. It is, not only the centre of our world, but also the life of this and the other planets which revolve round it, and which, did they not receive the warmth of his rays, would only be frozen solitudes. The Sun is indeed the origin of the energy displayed on the surface of this globe, and if not the source of everything living, is, at least, the supporter and feeder of life.

On the other hand, darkness is for man a symbol of death, and is always accompanied by all sorts of terrors which only vanish when the dawn appears. It is then that man awakes, and that he looks towards the East, and that when the radiant orb sheds its stream of light over fields and mountains, into the forests and the caves, that he falls down and pours out his soul in prayers, before the face of the *Almighty Agni*.

From this, it might be inferred that the worship of the Aryas was only that of deified matter. Such a view would however be wrong. In worshipping the different forces of Nature, the Arya saw in them not the only God, but some of his attributes, and beyond the Earth and the water, beyond the clouds and the winds, beyond the Sun and the Stars, he felt, he saw, he perceived there must be something, something distinct from all those, something greater than they, some unknown God, whom he called *Devadevas,* that is to say the *God of the Gods,* or *Prajapati,* the *Lord of Creatures,* and in a hymn to this supreme being the poet says: " Nothing existed " then, either visible or invisible. There was no supe" rior region ; no air; no heaven. Where was this " envelop of the World? In what bed was the water? " Where were those unfathomable depths of the air ?

" There was no death, no immortality. Nothing " announced the day or the night. He alone breathed, " without breath, enclosed in himself. He alone existed.

" In the beginning darkness was wrapped in darkness; " the water was without strength. All was a chaos. " The Being was in the midst of this chaos and this " great All was born through the warmth of his piety.

" In the beginning, love was in him, and from his intel" lect the first seed sprang. The wise (men), through " the work of the intellect, succeeded in forming the " union of the visible with the invisible.

. . . .
. . . . . " Who knows these things ? Who can " tell them ? Whence came the beings ? What is this " creation ? The gods have also been created by Him. " But he, who knows how he exists?

" He, who is the first author of this creation, supports " it. And what other could do it ? He, who from the " height of the heavens rests his eyes upon all this world, " alone knows it. What other could have this science ?"

This surely shows that the Polytheism of India about which so much has been said, was more apparent than real, and that if numerous idols were worshipped, if the sun and the stars were deified, they were not, at any rate, worshipped as the Devadevas.

After this brief survey of the "Rig-Veda" it remains to show that the worship it contains has not been confined to India only, but that it made its way to Europe, where it became the worship of the Greeks and subsequently of many other nations.

In the Greek mythology, we find the χαος which can easily be traced to the Sanskrit *kham*, a *vacuum*. Out of this χαος came the *Earth*, and the sky Ουρανος, the Sanskrit *Varuna*.

Rita seems to have become in Greek the fruitful Ρεια, whilst the *devas* can easily be assimilated to the Θεοι.

Saturnus, the *Sower*, and *Janus*, the *emblem of Nature*, are the same as *Savitri*, and *Jana* (from *jan* to produce).

The God of the Infernal Regions Αιδης, is the same as the invisible *Avitta* whilst Μινως reminds one of *Manu*.

The *Apollo* of the Greeks, also called Πυθιος, can be identified with *Buddha, the wise* (from *budh* to *know*); *Minerva*, with *Manasvini* (the *intelligent*); *Venus* with *Vanita* (loved), *Vulcanus* with *Ulka, a flame*, and *Vesta* with *Vastya*, a *hearth*.

The struggle between the Θεοι and the Τιτηνες, is very similar to that between the *Devas* and their enemies the *Daityas*, and last, but not least, the great Ζευς or Δις; or *Jupiter*, or *Deus*, is the same as the Sanskrit *Dyupati* or *divapati* (from *div* to *shine*) and Ζευς πατηρ or Δις πατηρ, in Latin *Jupiter*, are the same words as the Sanskrit *Dyupati* and *Divapati* (from *divya, celestial*, and *pati, lord* or *master*).

These comparisons might be extended to the whole of the Greek and Roman theology, but as the few names we have chosen are, we think, sufficient to show that the Greeks and the Hindoos, though now so far from each other, must have been in former ages, if not one nation, at least very near relations, we shall now proceed to examine the works of Sanskrit literature posterior to the "Rig-Veda."

Foremost among these are the *Sama Veda*, the *Yadjur Veda*, and the *Atharva Veda*.

These Vedas are the sacred books of the Brahmins, those they composed themselves, and as they contain a great deal which is to be found in the *Rig* I think it may safely be said that the first Veda was the work of poets and not of priests, and that it existed long before there was any well-defined form of worship.

The *Sama* contains the hymns of the *Rig* which were sung during the sacrifices, together with rules for chanting.

The *Yadjur Veda* is a collection of prayers and dissertations on several religious topics, and claims a share of our attention, because in it can be found many of the laws which afterwards formed the book of the *laws of Manu*.

The *Atharva Veda* is not probably so ancient as the other Vedas, and owing to the want of philosophical ideas, is not generally considered so valuable a work as the other sacred books, though invaluable to the student of history and philology. It contains numerous forms of exorcism, both in prose and in poetry, such as were used by the degenerated Brahmins, previous to the reform introduced in the worship of Brahma.

But if these three Vedas lack the interest of the *Rig*, they contain nevertheless what the *Rig* lacks, namely, *Mantras*, or *prayers—Brahmanas* and *Upanishads*, or Commentaries.

These *Upanishads* are philosophical books composed by

the Brahmins, and are appended to the sacred books, of which they form a part.

They are sometimes dialogues between a pupil and his master, sometimes dissertations pure and simple, and they always show that those who composed them, were true philosophers.

What could be more grand than the following *Upanishad* from the *Yadjur Veda*.

" He who is the primary cause " says the writer, " is " the fire, the sun, the air, the moon, the waters; he is " the pure Brahma, the lord of beings. All the moments " which measure time have sprung from his glittering " body, which no mortal can embrace or see either above, " or around, or in the centre. His glory is so great that " no image can represent it.

" It is He " say the Holy Scriptures " who was in the " golden egg, He before whom nothing was; it is He " who is the God of space, He who is the firstborn, He " who resides in the fruitful bosom, He who will be pro- " duced for ever.

" It is He who dwells in all beings under the endless " shapes He assumes. He before whom nothing was, He " who alone became everything. He the lord of beings " who delights in creating, made the three lights, the " Sun, the Moon, and the Fire; and his body has sixteen " limbs.

" To what God could we offer our sacrifices but to Him " who has made the air fluid and the earth solid, to Him " who has fixed the solar orb and the celestial space, and " who has spread the drops of rain in the air.

" To what God could we offer our sacrifices but to Him

"whom the heaven and earth mentally contemplate, whilst
"they are fortified and embellished by pious offerings,
"whilst they are illumined by the Sun which rolls above
"them, and fertilized by the waters which overflow them.

"The wise man rests his eyes upon this Mysterious
"Being, in whom the Universe, which has no foundation
"but Him, exists for ever. This world is in Him; it is
"from Him that this world came forth. He is inter-
"mingled and woven with all beings under the different
"shapes of existence. Therefore let the wise who knows
"all the secrets of Revelation, hasten to celebrate this
"Being whose existence is as mysterious as it is varied.
"He who knows His three states—Creation, Preservation
"and Destruction, wrapped in mystery, is united with
"the Father.

"This Brahma in whom spirits obtain immortality
"when they have reached the third region, is our true
"Father; all worlds and all beings are governed by
"Providence.

"Knowing the elements, knowing the worlds, knowing
"all regions, worshipping the word born first, the pious
"man embraces the vivifying spirit of the solemn sacri-
"fice by the meditation of his soul.

"Understanding that the heavens, the earth and the
"air are He only, knowing and perceiving that the worlds,
"that the space, and the solar orb are He only, he sees
"this supreme being, he becomes this being, he identifies
"himself with Him by achieving this vast and fruitful
"course of the solemn sacrifice.

"To obtain wealth and wisdom, I address my prayer
"to this admirable master of the *being* and *non-being*,
"friend of Indra, the fire which all creatures desire.

"' May this offering be efficacious! O Agni, make me
"' wise to-day, of this wisdom, which is adored by the gods
" and our forefathers. May this offering be efficacious!
"' May Agni and Prajapati grant me wisdom! May Indra
" and Vayu grant me wisdom! May Brahma give me
" reason! May both the priest and the warrior defend
" me! May the gods grant me extreme felicity. O
" thou who art that everlasting felicity, may this offering
" please thee, and be received by thee."

We shall end these remarks on the *Vedas* and their *Upanishads* by a translation of the legend of the *Universal deluge,* as found in the *Yadjur Veda.* It is interesting to compare it to the Biblical account, and though it is not here considered as a supernatural phenomenon, it nevertheless shows that there was in India, as well as in other countries, a tradition of this great cataclysm.

" In the morning the servants of Manu brought him
" water for the ablution, as when one brings it for the
" washing of hands. Manu having washed himself, a fish
" came into his hand, and this fish said to him these
" words: Protect me, and I shall save thee.—And from
" what wilt thou save me? A deluge shall destroy all
" the living creatures: I can save thee from this deluge.
" What protection do you need? The fish replied: So
" long as we are young, a great danger threatens us, for
" the fish do not spare the fish. In the first place thou
" shalt protect me by keeping me in a vase. When I
" shall have grown too big for this vase to contain me,
" thou shalt dig for me a basin, and thou shalt protect me
" by keeping me there; when I shall have grown too big
" for the basin, then thou shalt cast me into the sea: for

"from that time I shall be strong enough to defend my-
"self against all dangers.

"The fish soon became enormous, for it grew very
"quickly. Then the fish said: When the year in which
"this deluge is to take place shall be at hand, thou wilt
"be able, recollecting my advice, to prepare a ship, and
"when the deluge shall come, thou shalt go into the ship
"which thou shalt have constructed, and then I shall save
"thee.

"Manu having fed and protected the fish, cast it into
"the sea, and in that same year which the fish had indi-
"cated, he, mindful of the advice he had received, pre-
"pared his ship. When the deluge had come, he went
"into the ship. The fish came towards him swimming,
"and Manu fastened the cable of the ship to the horn of
"the fish, that he might lead it to the mountain of the
"North.

"Then the fish said: I have saved thee; now lash thy
"ship to a tree, in order that the water may not drag
"thee away, although thy ship is on a mountain. When
"the water shall have subsided, then thou wilt be able to
"come out of thy ship.

"Manu only came out when the water had abated, and
"it is from that, that comes the name which the mountain
"still retains—the coming down of Manu, coming out of
"his ship."

Then the writer goes on, and tells us that Manu offered a sacrifice, that a woman was formed out of the offering of milk, cheese and butter, and relates how that woman became the wife of Manu, and subsequently the second mother of mankind.

We cannot conclude this brief analysis of the sacred

books of India without alluding to the great reform which took place in the religion of *Brahma* about 800 years before our era. But before we say anything about this revolution in the old religion of India, it is necessary to state a few of the causes which led to this schism in the established worship.

The whole of the Aryas of India were divided into four *castes*, viz., the *Brahmins* or *priests;* the *Kshattras* or *warriors* (from *Kshi,* to *strike*); the *Vaishyas, colonists,* or *traders,* or *agriculturists,* from *vish,* to *occupy;* and the *Sudras,* or *servants,* from *sud,* to *purify.* These four castes were perfectly distinct from each other, and intermarriages were strictly prohibited by the Brahmins, who were not only the priests, but also the rulers of the nation. These Brahmins, resembling, in many respects, the priests of the Jews, had arrogated to themselves the management of civil and religious affairs, and having the law in their own hands, interpreted it so as to suit their own views. Belonging to the first of the four castes was not yet enough for them, they must be higher than the kings themselves; and in order to make people believe in their superiority over all other mortals, they did not hesitate to affirm that, before becoming Brahmins, they had been purified in a preceding life, and that their power was so great that not only could their words annihilate their enemies, but even create new worlds.

These falsehoods, being readily accepted by the people, had given the Brahmins a power which can only be compared to the one the Roman priests of the Middle Ages had in France, Spain, or Italy. Nevertheless this power, strong and deep-rooted as it was, was, if not destroyed, at least greatly weakened and diminished by a philosophy more in accordance with reason, and the progress the nation had made.

Sakya Muni was the propounder of the tenets of the new school.

Sakya Muni, or the *Buddha* (budh, to understand), was, it is said, the son of a mighty and wealthy prince, and of a mother remarkable for her beauty and purity. The first years of his life were spent, by him, in all the happiness fortune and rank can give.

He married a young girl, as beautiful as loving; he loved everybody, and everybody loved him; in short, nothing seemed to be wanting to make his bliss complete.

But this happiness did not last long; for when casting his eyes around him, when going in the midst of men, he found that there was woe, that there were misfortunes which he could not alleviate, miseries which he could not soothe, desires which gnawed at the very heart of men, and which he could not either appease or satisfy; and when, after having tried to find the means of rendering men happy, he discovered that he had laboured in vain, the cup of bliss was dashed from his lips. He, ashamed of being happy when others were suffering, leaves his palace, forsakes his loving spouse, gives up the pleasures and vanities of the world, and goes into the wilderness to lead the life of an anchorite. He had scarcely retired from the pomps of the world when the king of Maghada came to him, and by offering him the half of his kingdom, tried to induce him to relinquish his present mode of life. Having failed in attaining his object, the demon tried to win him, by employing the most powerful of tempters, viz., beautiful women whom the evil spirit sent to him, and who appeared before the *Buddha* in all their loveliness. But *Sakya Muni* once more remained victorious.

After having overcome these temptations, he went forth to preach to men the new religion.

He taught men that they were all equal, and that, contrary to the statements of the Brahmins, every man might become a priest, whatever his caste might be, provided he possessed the piety and learning qualifying him for the divine office. The favours of God which were only, till then, the lot of a few privileged ones, were to become the inheritance of all those who by their piety and charity should render themselves worthy of them.

Such is the teaching of the *Buddha*, a teaching which bears more than one point of resemblance to Christianity.

The *Buddha*, like Christ, was the friend of the oppressed, and the enemy of tyrants and hypocrites; his religion, like that of Christ, was also a religion of love, and the heavenly favours were to be confined no longer to one particular class, but within the reach of all.

If Buddhism has not completely destroyed Brahminism, it has at any rate shaken it to its very foundation; and if it is scarcely in existence in the country where it first was preached, Christianity is, no longer, the religion of Western Asia. Buddhism has travelled Eastward, and Christianity has shed its light over the Western nations; and they have under their banners more than one-half of mankind.

Some may object to this comparison, on the ground that Buddhism is a worship of Idols; but to this I shall reply, that if Buddhism is no longer the pure worship preached by *Sakya Muni*, Christianity, in many instances, is very far from what it was intended to be.

We must not be too sanguine in our condemnation of other worships; and before we criticize other people's conduct, we should examine our own.

If Buddhism has now become a worship of Idols, if its priests no longer remind one of the Great and Good *Buddha,* Christianity has more or less degenerated into a similar worship, whilst the virtues of its priests can no longer be compared to those of Christ.

Great is the number of those who pity the poor Buddhist who addresses his prayers to a worthless and unfeeling idol; but few are those who see that the Buddhist of China, prostrated before his idol, has thousands of imitators in Europe.

To see idols worshipped, we need not go to the far East, for only a few hours journey will show us what we should see thousands of miles away. When once we have set foot on the Continent of Europe we are in the midst of idols and images, as indeed any Catholic church will demonstrate. There we shall see hundreds kneeling before a plaster statue of a virgin, or before a reliquary containing some bones reputed to be those of a saint, and hundreds addressing their prayers to some still lower object, instead of invoking the only one God. Is not this Idolatry? Is not such a worship as demoralizing as modern Buddhism?

Those who laugh at the Buddhist because his sole desire, they say, is to be annihilated, have, I believe, been greatly mistaken.

The *Nirvana* of the Buddhist is not to be interpreted in the usual manner, for the desire of the Buddhist, like that of the Brahmin, is that his soul should become absorbed into that of the Deity, and not that it should

5 *

be utterly destroyed. The Buddhist prays for the annihilation of his body, but, like every other man, he hopes there is something after this life; and in several of the hymns of the Lalita Vistara, Buddha is asked to instruct his followers in order that they may become partakers of his immortality.

And now, we will say a few words about a work to which we have alluded before, namely, the *Manavadharma*, or the *law of Manu*. This book, composed at least a thousand years before our era, is a complete system of religious and civil legislation. In it are found all the laws which prescribe the duties and limit the rights of each caste; and such has been the influence of the *Manavadharma*, that after so many ages, and so many revolutions, its laws are not yet totally discarded by the Hindoos of the present day.

In the beginning of the *Manavadharma*, we are told that a luminous egg appeared in the water (the first substance), and that this egg, dividing itself, formed the heaven, the air, the earth, the fire, and the sea. Out of these elements came everything that grows or moves upon the surface of the earth, and also *Manu*, after the creation of which Brahma rested. Since then, everything has been submitted to Manu, who, for the guidance of his children, wrote the laws of the *Manavadharma*.

We cannot conclude this sketch of the literature of India, without noticing two poems which do not belong to the first caste, but to the *Kshattras* or *warriors*. These two poems are the *Ramayana*, written about eight hundred years before our era; and the *Mahábhárata*, which is two hundred years younger.

The *Ramayana*, composed by the poet *Valmiki*, contains

nearly 50,000 lines, and is a most precious and valuable monument of antiquity, and most valuable to the student of the history and customs of India.

The beginning of the poem shows us *Valmiki* meditating near the banks of a pure and calm river, when a voice from Brahma commanded him to celebrate the exploits of *Râma*. At once, the whole of the marvellous deeds of this renowned warrior passed before his mind, and *Valmiki*, inspired by the languid voices of two swans, began to recite before his disciples the poems which form the *Raymayana*.

To give an analysis of such an elaborate work is what we cannot attempt here, for the incidents are so plentiful that to relate them, even briefly, would fill a volume.

This poem, which can easily be likened to the great epics of Greece, shows once more that the same ideas have pervaded the whole of human nature. We find in it those Titans and Centaurs of Hesiod, whose deeds have also been recorded by Ovid; whilst *Rama* can advantageously be compared to Achilles or Æneas.

The other great Indian epic, the *Mahâbhârata*, is rather a collection of poems, by different authors, than the work of one man. This stupendous composition, containing about 200,000 lines, is the description of the great struggle which took place between the two branches of the royal family settled at *Hastinapura*, a struggle which ended in the ultimate victory of the virtuous *Yudhisthira*, son of *Pandus*, who had given his throne to his younger brother *Dhretarasta*, on condition that his son *Yudhisthira* should still retain the rights he had to the throne of his father.

In concluding this very imperfect sketch of so important and extensive a literature as that of India, I must express my regret that it is not more generally known in Europe; and I should esteem myself amply rewarded if these few pages should induce any one to begin the study of that language which has been the key to so many mysteries, and which is destined to throw more light on the Science of Religion than any other European language, namely, Sanskrit.

CHAPTER IV.

ETYMOLOGICAL VOCABULARY.

"There is something more truly wonderful in a root than in all the lyrics of the world."—*Prof. Max Müller*—"The Science of Language."

IN the following vocabulary, the English words, arranged for the sake of convenience, in alphabetical order, will be immediately followed by the Sanskrit root from which they have been derived.

Upwards of three hundred words are given, together with their roots, and although this may, at first sight, seem a very small quantum, considering the extensive vocabulary of the English language, yet, when the reader bears in mind that several derivatives are formed from one word, he will at once perceive that our Etymological Vocabulary, small as it is, supplies the etymologies of a very large number of English words. For instance, the etymology of the word *baker* will give that of *baking, bakery, bacon,* &c., whilst that of *spy* will supply the derivation of *special, species, specimen, specious, speck, spectacle, spectator, spectral, spectre, speculum,* and a host of others, such as *spite, despite, suspicion, suspect, prospect, expect, respect, respectable, auspicious,* and even *sceptic* and *Bishop*.

The Greek, Latin, French, or other foreign words given under the Sanskrit roots, are not always the translation of the English, though in many cases they are, but they are always words derived from the same source. It will also be noticed that sometimes the same word goes through several languages without undergoing any very material alteration in form, whilst in other cases, the spelling of a Greek word may be totally different from that of the English or German, and as, at first sight, one might think the roots have been given arbitrarily, it is necessary to mention some of the rules which regulate the changes letters undergo, in passing from one language into another.

Liquid and sibilant initials, in Sanskrit, remain unaltered throughout all Aryan languages, except Greek, where the breathings act as substitutes.

The mute consonants, which may be either *weak, strong,* or *aspirate,* undergo several remarkable changes.

The *weak,* in Sanskrit, Greek, Latin, or Russian becomes, in German, *strong;* the *strong, aspirate,* and the *aspirate, weak.*

The dental aspirated δ and ζ are wanting in Latin, Russian, and German, and in the latter language they generally become tz.

In the class of guttural letters, it must be noticed that the aspirated ones are neither found in English, nor in Latin, nor French, whilst they exist in German, Russian, and Greek, as well as some other European languages.

The labials are found to exist in all languages without undergoing any changes.

The French language, derived chiefly from the Latin, has dropped all the breathings used by the Gauls, and has only retained the abbreviations which were so common in the degenerated Latin spoken by their forefathers, and this accounts for the dropping of all the final vowels, in French.

OU has been changed into the French U; C has become K or S and G, GH or J; whilst CH is sometimes equivalent to the English SH and sometimes pronounced like a Latin C.

In English, we find that the vowels, in addition to the sounds they have in other languages, have been modified so that the same vowel has sometimes three or four different pronunciations; a fact which is explained by the nature of the English language itself, and which shows the influence that different idioms have upon a new language.

The Sanskrit V is equivalent to the Greek digamma which has been replaced by the *Spiritus Lenis*. In all other languages it is either the same as V or W.

The S initial is found in all tongues, but in Greek, the *spiritus asper* takes its place.

The Sanskrit D exists in Latin, French, Greek, and Russian, and becomes T in English, and T or Z in German.

The Sanskrit T corresponds to the Greek, Latin, French and Russian T, and becomes TH in English, and D or T in German.

The aspirate H is χ in Greek; H in Latin; Z in Russian; and G in German and English.

The Sanskrit SH is the same as the Greek κ, the Latin S, the Russian K or SH, and the English and German K, SC, SCH.

G is generally preserved throughout all languages, but at times becomes K, as in German, or C in English.

The Sanskrit J is equivalent to γ or ζ in Greek; to G in Latin and French; to K in German and English; and to z in Russian.

The Sanskrit M, used as an initial letter, is always the same, but when it is a final in Sanskrit, it becomes ν in Greek.

The Sanskrit B corresponds to the Greek β or ϕ; to the Latin and French B or F; and in other languages is frequently changed into P.

L is sometimes changed into R, though rarely.

The Sanskrit DH is equivalent to a soft English TH; and the T to a strong TH.

The German F is weakened into P in English, in words taken from the former language, and the German D becomes T in English.

The preceding laws being sufficient to elucidate the etymologies contained in the Vocabulary, we shall refer the reader, anxious to obtain further information on the subject, to philological works, which are too numerous and too well known to necessitate a special mention.

ETYMOLOGIES.

G. stands for German; F. for French; I. for Italian; Sp. for Spanish; L. for Latin; R. for Russian; and S. for Sanskrit. The Greek words, being all printed in Greek letters, are easily recognizable.

A

A—Un, *to reduce.*
G. ein. F. un. Sp. un. L. unus. S. una.

Ache—Ach, *to be hurtful.*
G. ach. ἀχος. S. anhas, *evil.*

All—Al, *to fill.*
G. alle. αλεις. S. ala, *many.*

Ant. (*prefix*), Ati, *before.*
G. ant. F. anté. I. and S. ante or anti. L. ante. αντι.

Ask—Isch, *to desire.*
G. heischen. L. egeo. ἰσχω. R. ishchu.

B

Bake—Pach, *to bake.*
G. backen. πεπτω. R. peku. S. pakti.

Baker—Pach, *to bake.*
G. bäcker. R. pechnik. S. pachaka, *a cook.*

Ball—Pail, *to throw.*
G. ball. F. balle. I. palla. Sp. bala.
L. pilum—βαλανος. S. pilu, *a dart.*

BAND—BANDH, *to tie.*

G. band. F. bande. I. benda. Sp. venda. S. bandha, *a tie.*

BARK—BARH, *to bark.*

G. bellen. R. burcu. βραχω.

BE—BHU, *to be born.*

G. bin. L. fuo. φυω. R. bywaiu.

BEAR—BHAR, *to bear.*

L. fero. φερω. R. beru. S. bhara, *burthen.*

BEAT—BADH, *to strike.*

G. besiegen. F. battre. I. battere. S. batir. L. batuo. πατεω. R. bodu. S. badha, *destructive.*

BETTER—BHAD, *to prosper.*

G. besser. S. bhadra.

BID—PATH, *to declare.*

G. bieten. L. peto. πειθω.

BIND—BANDH, *to tie.*

G. binden. F. bander. S. bandhas, a tie.

BITE—BHID, *to split.*

G. beissen.

BLADE—PHALL, *to open.*

G. blatt. F. feuille. L. folium. φυλλον. S. phulla, *a bud.*

BLEAT—BALH, *to bleat.*

G. blëken. F. bêler. I. belare. Sp. balar. L. balo. βληχαω. R. bleiu.

BLOOM—PHULL, *to blossom.*

G. bluhen. S. phullam, *a bud.*

BLOW—PVAL, *to move.*

G. blasen. L. flo. φλαω.

ETYMOLOGICAL VOCABULARY.

Bond—Bandh, *to tie.*
G. binden. S. baddah, *tied.*

Borough—Pur, *to fill.*
G. burg. F. bourg. I. borgo. Sp. burgo. πυργος. S. pura.

Bound—Bandh, *to tie.*
G. binden. S. baddha.

Bow—Bhuj, *to curve.*
G. bogen. πτυσσω. S. bhugna, *curved.*

Break—Bharv, *to break.*
G. brechen. F. briser. I. frangere. Sp. fracturar. L. frango. πριζω. S. brista, *broken.*

Brew—Bharj, *to fry.*
G. brauen. F. brasser. L. frigo. φρυγω. S. bhrinan.

Bride—Bhar, *to bear.*
G. braut. παρθενος. S. bhritâ.

Broad—Part, *to spread.*
G. breit. L. planum. πλατυς. S. partivi, *surface.*

Brother—Bhri, *to bear.*
G. bruder. F. frère. I. fratello. Sp. fraile. L. frater. φρατωρ. R. brat. S. bhratri.

Buck—Bukk, *to low.*
G. bock. F. bouc. I. becco. L. butio. βηκον. S. bukka, *a he-goat.*

C

Call—Kal, *to resound.*
G. klagen. L. clamo. καλεω. S. kala, *noise.*

Can—Jna, *to know.*
G. Kann. R. znaiu.

Chop—Chap, *to break.*

L. scindo. κοπτω. R. kopaiu.

Chough—Gu, *to murmur.*

F. Chouette. I. civetta. Sp. chucho. L. gemo. γοαω. S. guka.

Clang—Klad, *to moan.*

G. klang. F. cliquetis. L. clango. κλαζω. R. klishu.

Cock—Kuck, *to cry.*

F. coq. I. gallo. Sp. gallo. L. gallus. κικκὸς. S. kukkutta.

Cold—Jal, *to grow cold.*

G. kalt. L. gelidus. S. jala.

Cole—Chal, *to penetrate.*

G. kohl. I. cavolo. Sp. col. L. caulis. καυλὸς. R. kol. S. chula.

Come—Ga, *to move.*

G. kommen.

Cook—Kvath, *to cook.*

G. koch. F. cuisinier. I. cuoco. Sp. cocinero. L. coquo. S. kvathan, *boiling.*

Cool—Jal, *to grow cold.*

G. kühlen. L. gelo. R. cholozu.

Cow—Gu, *to low.*

G. kuh. L. gemo. γοαω. S. gau.

Crow—Kur, *to sing.*

G. krähen. F. corbeau. I. corvo. Sp. cuervo. L. corvus. κοραξ. S. karava.

Cuckoo—Kuck, *to scream.*

G. kuckuck. F. coucou. I. cuculo. Sp. cuco. L. cuculus. κοκκυξ. S. kaukila.

CUT—KASH, *to trench.*
G. kappen. F. couper. Sp. cortar. κεαζω.

D.

DAMP—DHU, *to move forward.*
G. dumpfig. θυμος. S. dhumah, *breath.*

DARE—DHARS, *to dare.*
G. dürfen. L. trux. θρασσω. R. derzaiu. S. dharsa, *boldness.*

DAUGHTER—DUH, *to draw.*
G. tochter. θυγατηρ. R. doch. S. duhitri.

DAY—DIV, *to shine.*
G. tag. Sp. dia. L. dies. R. den. S. diva.

DEAL—DAL, *to divide.*
G. theilen. L. dolo. δηλεω. R. dielu. S. dala, *a fragment.*

DEATH—TUD, *to destroy.*
G. tod. F. tuer. L. tumo. θυσια. S. tauda, *murder.*

DECK—TVATCH, *to cover.*
G. deck. F. toit. L. tectum. τεγος. S. tvatch, *a shelter.*

DEED—DHA, *to do.*
G. that. L. thesis. θεσις. S. datus, *a base.*

DEW—DHAI, *to drink.*
G. thau. θαω. R. doiu. S. daya.

DIM—TAM, *to obscure.*
G. dunkel. L. tabeo. τεμω. R. tmiu. S. tamasa, *darkened.*

DIP—TIP, *to damp.*

G. tauchen. F. tremper. δυπτω.

DIVINE—DIV, *to shine.*

F. divin. S. divya.

DO—DHA, *to do.*

G. thun. τιθημι. R. dieiu.

DOOR—DVAR, *to obstruct.*

G. thor. θυρα. R. dwer. S. dvar.

DREAM—DRAI, *to sleep.*

G. traümen. F. dormir. L. dormio. δαρθανω. R. dremliu.

DRIVE—TRAG, *to move.*

G. tragen. F. tirer. L. traho. τρεχω. R. trogaiu.

DRONE—DHRAN, *to hum.*

G. drohne. θρεω.

DRY—TARSH, *to dry.*

L. torreo. θερσω. S. tersa, *dryness.*

E.

EAR—AR, *to plough.*

L. arare. ἀρω. S. Arya.

EARTH—ARDH, *to become visible.*

G. erde. L. orior. ορομαι S. arddha, *fruitful.*

EAST—USH, *to glow.*

G. ost. F. est. I. est. S. este. L. oriens. αως and ἠῶς in Doric. S. ushâ, *the dawn.*

EAT—AD, *to eat.*

G. essen. L. edo. εδω. R. iem. S. atta, *eaten.*

Egg—Vi, *to pass,* or vi, *à bird.*
G. ei. F. œuf. I. uovo. S. huevo. L. ovum. ωον. R. iaico. S. vijam.

End—An, *to reach.*
G. ende. ἀνη. S. anta.

Err—Ir, *to go astray.*
G. irren. F. erreur. L. erro. ερρω. S. irana, *a desert.*

Ever—Ay, *to go.*
G. ewig. αιει. S. âyâu.

Ewe—Av, *to support.*
L. ovis. οἷς. R. owen. S. avi.

Eye—Aksh, *to spread.*
G. auge. F. œil. S. occhio. S. ojo. L. oculus. ὄκκος. R. oko. S. akshi.

F

Fail—Sphal, *to deviate.*
G. fehlen. F. faillir. I. fallare. Sp. faltar. L. fallo. σφαλλω.

Fall—Sphal, *to deviate.*
G. fallen.

Fallow—Pal, *to pass.*
G. falb. F. fauve. S. flavo. L. pullus. πωλος.

Fang—Pach, *to hold.*
G. fang. L. pango. πηγνυω. R. pagu. S. pachas, *a tie.*

Far—Par, *to advance.*
G. fern. L. prius. παρος. S. pura, *formerly.*

FARE—PAR, *to advance.*
G. fahren. περαω.

FATHER—PÂ, *to nourish.*
G. vater. F. père. I. padre. Sp. padre. L. pater. πατηρ. R. batia. S. pitri.

FEAR—BRI, *to fear.*
G. fürchten. L. frigeo. φρισσω.

FEATHER—PAT, *to fly.*
G. feder. L. penna. πτερον. patram, *a wing.*

FEED—PU, *to take care of.*
F. futtern. F. paître. I. pascere. Sp. pacer. L. pasco. παω. R. pascu. paushana, *food.*

FEW—PAY, *to decline.*
F. peu. I. poco. Sp. poco. L. paucus. παυω. S. payga, *weak.*

FIGHT—PISCH, *to wound.*
G. fechten. L. pugno. πεικω. R. pichaiu. S. pinja, *a blow.*

FILL—PALL, *to increase.*
G. fullen. L. plenus. πλεω. R. polniu.

FIRE—PRUSH, *to burn.*
G. feuer. F. feu. I. fuoco. Sp. fuego. L. febris. πυρ. R. pariu. S. prausha, *combustion.*

FISH—PI, *to drink.*
G. fisch. F. poisson. I. pesce. Sp. pez. L. piscis. S. pasasya, *aqueous.*

FLEE—PLIH, *to move onward.*
G. fliehen. πλισσω.

Flow—Plu, *to float.*

G. fliessen. I. fluire. Sp. fluir. L. fluo. φλύω. plavan, *running.*

Foal—Bal, *to live.*

G. fohlen. S. bâla, *a child.*

Foot—Pad, *to walk.*

G. fuss. F. pied. I. pie. Sp. pie. L. pes. πους. S. pad.

For—Prati, *towards.*

G. für. F. pour. I. per. Sp. por. L. pro. προς.

Fore—Pra, *before.*

G. vor. F. pré. L. prae. πρω.

Friend—Pri, *to delight.*

G. freund. L. prurio. R. priatnyi. S. prita, *beloved.*

Full—Pall, *to increase.*

G. voll. L. plenus. πολυς. R. polnyi.

G

Gait—Ga, *to walk.*

G. gang. S. gati, *a way*

Gird—Gar, *to enclose.*

G. gürten. L. gyro. γυροω. R. gorod. S. gerha- enceinte.

Glee—Hil, *to enjoy.*

κλειω. S. haili, *gaiety.*

Glow.—Jval, *to blaze.*

G. gluth. F. chaleur. L. caleo. κηλεοω. R. kaliu. S. jvala, *burning.*

Go—Ga, *to walk.*

G. gehen. L. cio. κιω. S. gati, *a way.*

Good—Huth, *to whiten.*

G. gut. S. hutha, *pure.*

Goose—Has, *to laugh.*

G. gans. Sp. ganso. L. anser. χην. R. gus. S. hansa.

Greedy—Gardh, *to desire.*

G. gierig. S. gardhu.

H

Hair—Char, *to pierce.*

G. haar. L. crinis. κορση. S. chirsam, *a crest.*

Hall—Chal, *to enclose.*

G. halle. F. salle. L. sacellum. αυλα. R. zala. S. Châlâ.

Hand—Han, *to touch.*

G. hand. S. hasta.

Hard—Kar, *to act.*

G. hart. κρατος. S. kratu, *strong.*

Hare—Shash, *to spring up.*

G. hase. R. zaec. S. shasha.

Hate—Hath, *to hate.*

G. hassen. F. haïr. L. irascor. εριζω. S. irsha, *hatred.*

Have—Ap, *to hold.*

G. haben. F. avoir. I. avere. Sp. haber. L. habeo. απτω. S. apta, *held.*

Heat—Indh, *to burn.*

G. hitze. L. ardor. αιθος. S. aidha.

Heart—Harsh, *to be moved.*

G. herz. F. cœur. I. Cor. Sp. corazon. L. cor. καρδια. S. hardaya.

Heir—Har, *to seize.*

G. erbe. F. héritier. I. erede. Sp. heredero. L. haeris. S. hara.

Hew—Hau, *to cut.*

G. hauen. R. huiu.

Hide—Kud, *to cover.*

G. haut. L. cutis. χρὼς. Kudi, *envelope.*

High—Uch, *to increase.*

G. hoch. F. haut. L. altus. S. uchcha.

Hold—Hul, *to cover.*

G. hülle

Hollow—Hal, *to dig.*

G. hohl. R. koliŭ. S. halin, *husbandman.*

Holm—Kul, *to heap up.*

G. holm. L. culmen. κολωνος. R. cholm. S. kulan.

Hope—Kup, *to be passionate.*

G. holfen. καπυω. S. kupian, *passionate.*

Horn—Char, *to pierce.*

G. horn. F. corne. I. corno. Sp. cuerno. L. cornu. κερας. S. cherni.

Hound—Kan, *to resound.*

G. hund. L. canis. κύων. S. kuna.

House—Kud, *to cover.*

G. haus. I. casa. Sp. casa. L. casa. S. kuta.

Hurry—Char, *to reach.*

L. curro. χορος. S. chara, *motion.*

Hut—Kud, *to cover.*

G. hütte. F. hutte. L. casa. κευθος. S. kuti.

I

In—An, like the *a* privative.

G. un. F. in. I. in. Sp. en. L. in. αν or α.

Iron—Ay, *to run through.*

G. eisen. F. fer. I. ferro. Sp. hierro. L. æes. S. ayasa.

Is—As, *to be.*

G. ist. F. est. I. e. Sp. es. L. est. εστι. R. est. S. asti.

J

Joke—Jaks, *to laugh.*

Sp. chancear. L. jocor.

K

Keep—Kumb, *to spread.*

L. capio. κυπτω. R. kopliu.

Kin—Jan, *to produce.*

L. genus. γενος. S. kana.

Kind—Jan, *to produce.*

G. kind. I. genere. Sp. genero. L. genitus. γενναω. S. janita, *born.*

King—Jan, *to produce.*

G. könig. S. jana, *a man.*

Knee—Jya, *to bend.*

G. knie. F. genou. I. ginocchio. L. genu. γονυ. S. jânu.

Know—Jna, *to know.*

G. kennen. F. connaître—I. conoscere. Sp. conocer. L. cognosco. γινοσκω. R. gnaiu.

L

Lay—Lag, *to adhere.*
G. legen. L. loco. λοχαω. R. lozu.

Leap—Laip, *to spring forth.*
G. laufen. λειπω.

Less—Lich, *to diminish.*
G. loss. L. laevus. λαιος. S. laicha, *weak.*

Let—Lich, *to diminish.*
G. lassen. F. laisser. I. lasciare. L. liceo. λιαζω. R. lisaiu.

Lewd—Lubh, *to desire.*
G. lüderlich. F. licencieux. I. libidinoso. Sp. lascivo. L. laxivus. λαγνος. S. laubha, *passion.*

Lick—Lib, *to lick.*
G. lecken. F. lécher. I. leccarsi. Sp. lamer. L. lingo. λειχω. R. lizu.

Lie—Lî, *to adhere.*
G. liegen. L. lego. λεγω. R. lezu. S. lagna, *adherent.*

Light—Laksh, *to appear.*
G. licht. F. lumière. I. lume. Sp. luz. L. lumen, or lucerna. λυχνος. S. lauchaya, *shining.*

Lion—Lu, *to cut up.*
G. löwe. F. lion. I. leone. Sp. leon. L. leo. λεων. S. lunan, *a wild beast.*

Look—Lauk, *to see.*
L. lucco. λευσσω. S. lauka, *sight.*

Lop—Lup, *to cut off.*
G. kappen. λυπεω. R. lupliu. S. laupa, *a wound.*

Lose—Lup, *to cut off.*
G. lösen. L. luo. λυω. R. lozzu.

Love—Lubh, *to desire, or to love.*
G. lieben. L. libeo. λιππω. R. liubliu.

Love—Lubh, *to desire, or to love.*
G. liebe. R. liubow. S. laubha, *passion.*

Lust—Las, *to enjoy.*
G. lust. L. lusus. λαφυσσω. S. lasa.

M

Mad—Mad, *to intoxicate.*
I. matto. L. mitis. ματαιος. S. matta.

Make—Mak, *to act.*
G. machen. Sp. maquinar. L. machinor. μηχανωμαι.

Man—Man, *to think.*
G. mann. R. muz. S. manu.

Matter—Mâ, *to bring forth.*
G. Materie. F. matière. I. materia. Sp. materia. L. materia. S. matra, *a substance.*

Mead—Mad, *to intoxicate.*
G. meth. μεθυ. R. mëd. S. madu, *a liquor.*

Mete—Mâ, *to measure.*
G. mass. F. mesurer. I. misurare. Sp. medir. L. metior. μετρεω. R. mezuiu.

Middle—Mid, *to conciliate.*
G. mitte. F. milieu. I. mezzo. Sp. medio. L. medius. μεσος. R. mezen. S. madhya.

Midge—Muj, *to hum.*
G. mücke. F. mouche. I. mosca. Sp. mosca. L. musca. μυια. R. mucha. S. makshika.

Might—Mah, *to prevail.*

G. macht. L. majestas. μεγεθος. R. moguta. S. mahatva, *power.*

Mild—Mul, *to compress.*

G. mild. F. mou. I. molle. Sp. mole. L. mollis. μαλακος. R. mylii. S. malita, *compressed.*

Mind—Man, *to think.*

G. meinung. I. mente. Sp. mente. L. mens. μητις. S. mati, *intellect.*

Mix—Mishr, *to mix.*

G. mischen. F. mêler. I. mischiare. Sp. mezclar. L. misoeo. μισγω. R. miesaiu. S. mishra, *mixed.*

Moil—Mal, *to tarnish.*

G. mal. L. mollesco. μολυνω. S. mala, *soiled.*

Monk—Mû, *to seclude.*

G. mönch. F. moine. I. monaco. Sp. monge. L. monachus. μοναχὸς. S. muni, *solitary.*

Month—Mâ, *to measure.*

G. monat. F. mois. I. mese. Sp. mes. L. mensis. μὴν. S. masa.

Mood—Maid, *to reflect.*

G. muth. F. mode. I. modo. Sp. modo. L. modus. μηδος.

Moon—Mâ, *to measure.*

G. mond. F. mois. L. mensis. μηνη. R. miesiac. S. mas.

Mother—Ma, *to bring forth.*

G. mutter. F. mère. I. madre. Sp. madre. L. mater. μητηρ. R. mat. S. matri.

Mouse—Mush, *to cut.*

G. maus. L. mus. μυς. R. mys. S. mûsha.

Mow—Mush, *to cut.*

G. mähen. I. metere. L. mutilo. μασσω. R. miku.

Much—Mah, *to prevail.*

G. manch. I. molto. Sp. mucho. L. magnus. μεγας. R. mnogii. S. mahat, *great.*

Murder—Mar, *to die.*

G. mord. F. meurtre. L. mors. μορος. R. Smert. S. mara, *death.*

N

Nail—Nakk, *to pierce.*

G. nagel. F. ongle. L. unguis. ονυξ. R. nagot. S. naka.

Name—Jna, *to know.*

G. name. F. nom. I. nome. Sp. nombre. L. nomen. ὄνομα. S. naman.

Naval—Nu, *to flow.*

F. naval. I. navale. Sp. naval. L. navis. ναυς. S. navya.

Navel—Nabh, *to penetrate.*

G. nabel. L. umbo. S. nabhi.

New—Ni, *to move.*

G. neu. F. neuf. I. nuovo. Sp. nuevo. L. novus. νεος. R. nowyi. S. nava.

Nigh—Nah, *to join.*

G. nahe. L. neo. νηω. S. naha, *cohesion.*

NIGHT—NACH, *to destroy.*
G. nacht. F. nuit. I. notte. Sp. noche. L. nox. νυξ. R. noch. S. nich.

NO—NA, *privative particle, like* No.
G. nein. F. non or ne. I. no. Sp. no. L. ne. νη.

NOSE—NAS, *to project.*
G. nase. F. nez. I. naso. Sp. nariz. L. nasus. R. nos. S. nas.

O

OF—AVA, *far or out of.*
G. ab. F. ab. L. ab. απω.

OLD—AL, *to fill.*
G. alt. L. altus. S. alita.

ONE—UN, *to reduce.*
G. eins. F. un. I. uno. Sp. uno. L. unus. S. unas.

ON—ANU, *on, or upon.*
G. an. L. ad. ava.

OUT—UT, *out.*
G. aus.

OVER—UPARI, *upon or above.*
G. über. L. super. υπερ.

OWE—ISH, *to possess.*
ισχω.

P

PATH—PATH, *to walk.*
G. pfad. F. passage. L. passus. πατος. R. put. S. patha.

Pawn—Pan, *to negotiate.*

G. pfanden. πονος. S. pana, *a transaction.*

Pit—Put, *to stand close together.*

G. pfuhl. F. puits. I. plateo. Sp. patio. L. puteus. βυθος. S. pauta, *bottom.*

Pool—Pal, *to pass.*

G. pfuhl. I. palude. L. palus. πηλος. S. palvala.

Q

Quack—Kuch, *to shout.*

G. quacksalber. L. clamo. κρακτικος. R. kokuiu.

Queen—Jan, *to produce.*

G. königin. γυνη. R; gena. S. jani, *a woman.*

Quick—Chak, *to prosper.*

κικυς. S. chaka.

Quiet—Chi, *to repose.*

I. quieto. Sp. quieto. L. quietus. κοιτος. S. chayatta.

Quoth—Kath. *to say.*

κοαω. R. koiu.

R

Radius—Râj, *to radiate.*

G. radius. F. rayon. I. raggio. Sp. radio. L. radius. ραβδος. S. rajis.

Rage—Raj, *to colour.*

G. rasen. F. rage. I. rabbia. Sp. rabia. L. rabies. ραγω. S. rajas, *passion.*

Rain—Ray, *to flow.*

G. regen. L. rivus. ραινω. S. rayas, *flood.*

REACH—RAJ, *to dominate.*

G. reichen. L. rego. ρεζω.

REAP—RIP, *to pluck up.*

L. rumpo. ρεπω.

RED—RAJ, *to colour.*

G. roth. F. rouge. I. rosso. Sp. rubio. L. ruber. ερυθρος. S. rakta.

RISE—RUH, *to grow.*

G. reisen. L. ruo. ρωω. R. rozu. S. rudis, *growth.*

RIVER—RI, *to flow.*

F. rivière. I. riviera. Sp. rio. ρεω. S. ritis.

ROB—RIP, *to pluck up.*

G. rauben. I. rubare. Sp. robar. L. rapio. ριπτω. R. rubliu. S. raipas.

ROD—RÂJ, *to radiate.*

ραβδος. S. radis.

RUN—RI, *to flow.*

G. rennen. L. ruo. ραινω. R. rieiu.

RUSH—RAS, *to grumble.*

G. rauschen. L. rugio. ροιζεω. R. rychu. S. râsa, *a noise.*

S

SAME—SAM, *to unite.*

G. selb. L. similis. R. samyi. S. sama, *equal.*

SAW—SACH, *to saw.*

G. sägen. F. scier. I. segare. Sp. serrar. L. seco. R. sieku.

SCATH—SKAD, *to hurt.*

G. schade. σκεδαω.

Sea—Su, *to spring up.*
G. see.

Seam—Siv, *to sew.*
G. saum. F. suture. L. sutura. S. simam.

Seat—Sad, *to sit down.*
G. sitz. F. siege. I. sedia. Sp. silla. L. sedes. εδρα. S. sadas.

Seed—Su, *to produce.*
G. saat. F. semence. I. seme. Sp. semilla. L. satus. S. sutis.

Seek—Sach, *to follow.*
G. suchen. F. chercher. L. sequor.

Serpent—Sarp, *to creep.*
G. schlange. F. serpent. I. serpente. Sp. serpiente. L. serpens. ερπετος. S. sarpa.

Sew—Siv, *to sew.*
L. suo. R. siiu. S. sutas, *sewed.*

Shade—Schad, *to veil.*
G. schatten. F. ombre. I. ombra. Sp. sombra. L. scena. σκιαζω. S. schadi, *a shelter.*

Shear—Kshur, *to shave.*
G. scheren. ξυραω. S. kshurin, *a barber.*

Shine—Chad, *to shine.*
G. scheinen. L. cremo. καιω.

Shoot—Skad, *to emerge.*
G. schiessen. L. scando. σκαζω.

Shut—Sku, *to enclose.*
G. schliessen. σκεπω.

ETYMOLOGICAL VOCABULARY.

Sister—Sva, *beloved,* and Stri, *wife.*
G. schwester. F. sœur. L. soror. R. sestra. S. svasri.

Sit—Sad, *to sit down.*
G. setzen. F. s'asseoir. I. sedere. Sp. sentarse. L. sedeo. εξομαί. R. sizu.

Sleep—Svap, *to sleep.*
G. schlafen. F. sommeil. L. somnus. υπνος. R. spanie. S. svapna.

Smart—Smar, *to remember.*
G. schmerzen. S. smara, *remembrance.*

Smile—Smi, *to smile.*
F. sourir. L. subrideo. μείδαω. R. smieiu. S. smita, *irony.*

Snow—Sna, *to water.*
G. schnee. F. neige. L. nix. νίφος. R. snieg. S. suava, *a shower.*

Soak—Sich, *to moisten.*
G. saugen. L. sugo. R. sosu. S. saika, *liquid.*

Society—Saj, *to join.*
F. société. L. societas. σαγη. S. sakta, *joined.*

Son—Su, *to produce.*
G. sohn. ἱυίς. R. syn. S. sûnu or suta.

Sound—Svan, *to resound.*
G. sund. F. son. I. suono. Sp. sonido. L. sonus. R. zwon. S. svana.

Sow—Su, *to produce.*
G. säen. F. semer. I. seminare. Sp. sembrar. L. sero. σευω. R. sieiu.

SPHERE—SPHAR, *to brandish.*
G. sphäre. F. sphère. σφαίρα. S. sphara, *rotation.*

SPREAD—SPHAR, *to brandish.*
G. spreiten. L. pargo. σπείρω. S. sphara, *ratation.*

SPY—PASCH, *to look.*
G. späher. F. espion. I. spia. Sp. espia. L. spicio. σκεπτω. S. spaschas.

SQUIRREL—SCHAD, *to cover.*
F. écureuil. I. scoiatto. L. sciurus. σκιουρος.

STAMP—STABH, *to fix.*
G. stampfen. F. estamper. I. stampare. S. estampar. L. stipo. στείβω. R. stupaiu.

STAND—STHA, *to stand.*
G. stehen. L. sto. σταω. R. staiu. S. Sthas, *fixed.*

STAR—STAR, *to spread.*
G. stern. I. stella. Sp. estrella. L. stella. αστρον. S. star.

STEER—STA, *to stand.*
G. stier. Sp. toro. L. taurus. Sp. sturas.

STEM—STABH, *to fix.*
G. stam. L. stirps. στυπος. S. stambha, *stump.*

STICK—STHAG, *to obstruct.*
G. stecken. στεγω.

STIGMA—TIG, *to penetrate.*
G. schimpf. F. stigma. L. stigma. στιγμα. S. tigma, *a sting.*

STING—STAK, *to prick.*
G. stechen. στιζω. R. stegaiu. S. tigma, *a sting.*

STONE—STHA, *to stand.*
G. stein. στυλος. Sthuna, *a pillar.*

STOOL—STHAL, *to place.*
G. stuhl. R. stul. S. sthala.

STOW—STAI, *to enclose.*
G. stauen. στυω. S. stana, *compact.*

STREET—STAR, *to spread.*
G. strasse. I. strada. L. stratum. στωτον. S. strata.

STREW—STAR, *to spread.*
G. streuen. L. sterno. στρωω. R. stroiu.

STRIKE—STARH, *to strike.*
G. streichen. L. stringo. στραγγω.

STUPID—STUBH, *to condense.*
F. stupide. L. stupidus. στυφρος. Stubdhas, *thick.*

SUN—SU, *to produce.*
G. some. F. soleil. I. sole. Sp. sol. L. sol. S. sunus.

SWEAT—SVID, *to perspire.*
G. schweis. F. sueur. I. sudore. Sp. sudor. L. sudor. S. svaida.

SWEET—SVAD, *to taste.*
G. siiss. F. suave. I. soave. Sp. suave. L. suavis. S. svadu.

T

TAKE—TIG, *to reach.*
S. tomar. L. tango. ταγγω. R. tykaiu. S. tiktas, *reached.*

TAME—DAM, *to tame.*
G. zähmen. F. dompter. L. domo. δαμαω. S. dama, *tamer.*

7

TAP—TUP, *to strike gently.*
G. zapfen. F. taper. Sp. tocar. τυπτω. R. topaiu.

TEACH—DISH, *to indicate.*
G. zeigen. L. disco. δεικω—δειξω. S. dishta, *taught.*

TEAR—DAR, *to split.*
G. zerren. L. tero. τειρω. R. deru. S. dâri, *a cut.*

TEN—DASH, *to cut off.*
G. zehn. F. dix. I. dieci. Sp. diez. L. decem. δεκα. R. desiat. S. dashan.

TEPID—TAP, *to warm.*
F. tiĕde. I. tepido. Sp. tibio. L. tepidus. R. teplyi. S. tapan, *warm.*

TERRIFY—TRAS, *to tremble.*
F. terrifier. I. atterire. Sp. aterrar. L. terreo. ταρασσω. R. triasu. S. trastas, *terrified.*

THIN—TAN, *to stretch.*
G. dünn. L. tenuis. ταναος. R. tonkyi. S. tanu.

THINK—DHI, *to conceive.*
G. denken. δοκεω. S. dyanam, *reflection.*

THIRST—TARSH, *to dry.*
G. durst. L. torris. θερος. S. tarsha.

THREE—TÂR, *to intercalate.*
G. drei. F. trois. I. tre. Sp. tres. τρεις. R. tri. S. tri.

THROUGH—TÂR, *to penetrate.*
G. durch. F. à travers. L. trans. S. tiras.

THUNDER—TAN, *to stretch.*
G. donner. F. tonnerre. I. tuono. Sp. trueno. L. tonitru.

TINE—DAU, *to divide.*
G. zinke. F. dent. L. dens. ὀδους. S. danta.

TO—ADI, *towards.*
G. zu. F. de. L. de.

TOWN—DHA, *to place.*
L. domus. δωμα. S. dhaman.

TREAD—TRAD, *to press.*
G. treten. F. trépigner. L. trudo. τρεω.

TREMBLE—TRAS, *to agitate.*
G. zittern. F. trembler. L. tremo. τρεμω.

TRUST—DARS, *to defy.*
G. trauen. L. trux. θρασυς. S. darsu.

TUG—DUH, *to draw.*
G. ziehen. L. duco.

TUMULT—TAM, *to disturb.*
F. tumulte. L. tumultus. S. tumulas.

TUNE—TAN, *to stretch.*
G. ton. F. ton. I. tuono. Sp. tono. L. tonus. τονος. S. tana.

TUTOR—TAY, *to protect.*
F. tuteur. L. tutor. τεττα. R. tiatia. S. tata, *patron.*

TWO—DAU, *to divide.*
G. zwei. F. deux. I. due. Sp. dos. L. duo. δυω. R. dwa. S. dvi.

U

UDDER—AID, *to swell.*
G. enter. L. uber. ουθαρ. S. uda.

7 *

UN—AN, *the same as a privative.*
G. un. F. in. L. in. αν. ava.

UNDER—ANTAR, *in or between.*
G. unter. F. entre. L. inter. εντος.

UP—UPA, *near.*
G. auf. υπω.

V

VIRILE—VÎR, *to defend.*
F. viril. L. virilis. S. varas, *a warrior.*

VISCOUS—VIS, *to spill.*
F. visqueux. I. viscovo. Sp. viscoso. L. virus. S. visa, *poison.*

VOICE—VACH, *to speak.*
F. voix. I. voce. Sp. voz. L. vox. ηχεω. S. vach, *voice.*

W

WAG—VAJ, *to move.*
G. wedeln. L. veho. οχεω.

WAGGON—VAJ, *to move.*
G. wagen. L. vehes. ὄχος. R. wezenie. S. vahanam.

WAIST—VAS, *to cover.*
F. veste. L. vestis. ἐσθής. S. vasta.

WALK—VALG, *to turn.*
G. walken. ελκω. R. woloku.

WALL—VALL, *to protect.*
G. wand. L. vallis. S. valla, *a rampart.*

WAR—VIR, *to defend.*

L. vis. ἰσχυς.

WAS—VAS, *to be.*

G. war. S. vasu.

WASTE—VAST, *to destroy.*

G. wüste. L. vastatus. αταω. S. vastita, *destroyed.*

WATER—UD, *to flow.*

G. wasser. L. unda. ὑδορ. R. woda. S. udam.

WAVE—VAH, *to carry.*

G. woge. F. vague. S. vaha.

To WAVE—VAISS, *to tremble.*

G. weben. L. vibro.

WAY—VAH, *to carry.*

G. weg. L. via. S. vahas.

WEATHER—VA, *to blow.*

G. wetter. L. ventus. αητης. R. wieter. S. vatri.

WEAVE—VAP, *to weave.*

G. weben. S. vapus, *a woven stuff.*

WEED—VAI, *to entangle.*

L. vitis. ἰτεα. R. wietu. S. vaitra, *a stem.*

WEB—VAP, *to weave.*

G. geweben. S. vapus, *a woven stuff.*

WELL—VIL, *to cover.*

G. wohl. L. validus. S. vallita, *compact.*

WEST—VAS, *to cover.*

G. west. F. ouest. L. vesper. εσπερος. S. vasati, *shade.*

WHEEL—VAIL, *to turn.*

L. volvo. ειλεω. R. walia.

WICK—VISH, *to occupy.*
L. vicus. οικος. R. wes. S. vaishas.

WIDOW—VI, *without* DHAVA, *husband.*
G. witwe. F. veuve. I. vedova. Sp. vidua. L. vidua. S. vidhava.

WIFE—VAP, *to weave.*
G. weib.

WILL—VAL, *to choose.*
G. willen. F. vouloir. I. volere. L. velle. βουλομαι. R. woliu.

WIND—VA, *to blow.*
G. wind. F. vent. I. vento. Sp. vento. L. ventus. αητης. S. vatis.

WISH—VASH, *to desire.*
G. wünsch. F. vœu. I. voto. Sp. voto. L. votum. S. vasha.

WIT—VID, *to discern.*
G. witz. L. video. ειδεω. R. witzu. S. vidvas, *learned.*

WOLF—VARK, *to seize.*
G. wolf. L. vorax. R. wilk. S. vrika.

WOMB—VAM, *to vomit.*
G. waume. L. vomo. εμεω. S. vama, *bosom.*

WOO—VASH, *to desire.*
G. weihen. F. vouer. L. voveo.

WORD—VART, *to become.*
G. wort. L. verbum. S. vritha, *rhythm.*

WORK—WIJ, *to act.*
G. werk. εργον. S. urja, *effort.*

WORTH—VAR, *to prefer.*

G. werth. R. wiernyi. S. vritya, *acceptable.*

Y

YOKE—YUJ, *to join.*

G. joch. F. joug. I. giogo. Sp. yugo. L. jugum. ζυγον. R. igo. S. yugam.

YOUNG—YU, *to increase.*

G. jung. F. jeune. I. giovane. Sp. joven. L. juvenis. R. iunyi. S. yuvan.

CHAPTER V.

Classification of Language.

The first philologists who ever attempted to classify the different languages into Branches or families, took a certain quantity of words belonging to different parts of speech, in a particular tongue, and having translated them into the corresponding words, in several other tongues, based their classification upon the similitude which was found to exist between different idioms.

The result of this comparison was, that some tongues which belong to very different classes, were considered as members of the same family, whilst others, which in reality are cognate, were pointed out as belonging to a branch of language with which they really have no affinity.

So long therefore, as the above was the only standard of comparison, very little advance was made towards a scientific classification of language.

As we have seen before, the discovery of Sanskrit had been a revelation, and it was also from the ancient language of India that the true method of comparing was to arise.

Frederick Schlegel, in his work on the "Language and Wisdom of the Indians" pointing out what great results were to be expected from a thorough knowledge of

Sanskrit, laid the foundation stone on which the new Science of Comparative Grammar was built.

The first work of importance, published on the subject, was the "Comparative Grammar of Sanskrit, Greek, Latin, Persian, and German tongues" by Francis Bopp, a work which was only a kind of introduction to his "Great Comparison of the Grammar of Sanskrit with that of Zend, Greek, Latin, Slavonic, Lithuanian, Gothic, and German."

Other eminent scholars soon followed in the same path and the names of Humboldt, Schlegel, Grimm, Burnouf, Max Müller, Eichhoff, are for ever associated with the science of Comparative Philology.

Then, the classification of language no longer consisted in lists of words, which as we shall see, were not sufficient to establish a criterion of relationship between two languages, but their grammatical forms became the distinguishing mark.

A likeness between the words does not indeed prove that any affinity exists between two tongues; for if this were so we might be induced to believe that Chinese, Sanskrit, and Hebrew are cognate languages.

Many Chinese words are not indeed, very unlike some Sanskrit ones; for instance, *vòu* and *vajas* (force or strength), *piào* and *pat* (to steal), *ping* and *pana* (trouble), or the Hebrew *avah* and the Sanskrit *val, to be willing*; and yet we know that far from belonging to the same family, they each form a special type, and are members of three different families. And what constitutes this difference, is the grammar of these languages only.

It is therefore, by comparing the different forms speech assumes in different dialects, that we are enabled to lay down the rules which must be followed in the classification of languages, rules which are always subjected to the great law of the Phonetic change of letters, discovered by Grimm.

Comparative Grammar serves, not only to divide language into great families, but also to arrange them in classes and branches, for although the languages of one family exhibit in their grammar many points of similitude, yet in some respects, they differ more or less from the original pattern of grammar, and as some always show the same difference they may be placed together so as to form a class which in its turn, and for the reason just mentioned, may necessitate to be subdivided into branches.

Thus, if English and French are compared with one another, it will be at once found that their respective grammars have been cast into the same mould, namely, the Sanskrit Grammar. It will also be seen that many thousands of words are the same in the two languages we have chosen, but on further inquiry it will be discovered that the Grammar of the English language is peculiar to a group of languages, which we call the "Low German branch," whilst that of the French has been copied on the Grammar of the Latin language.

Had it not been for Comparative Grammar, many languages could never have been classified; such is, for instance, the English language, in whose dictionary are found words which have been borrowed from nearly every language spoken on Earth. It abounds in French, Latin, Greek, German, and Italian words and expressions, as well as in Spanish, Portuguese, Arabic, Dutch, Chinese, and even Polynesian terms.

Now that we have summarily alluded to the method of

comparison now in use, we shall proceed to explain the genealogical table found at the end of this chapter.

In the first chapter of this book we have enumerated the reasons which have induced us to conclude that all languages of mankind have sprung from one common stock, and though a great deal may be said both in favour and against the theory of the "Common Origin of Language," yet as it has never been proved impossible that mankind should have been originally of one speech, whilst, on the other hand, no plausible argument can be brought forward in support of the adverse theory, we shall continue to consider all the different idioms of the world as the offspring of a common parent.

Upon this fact, or, at any rate, probability, we have constructed our "Genealogical Table," from which it will be seen that from the *Primitive Language* three families of speech have sprung, viz. :—

1. The *Aryan,* or *Indo-European Family.*
2. The *Semitic,* or *Syro-Arabian.*
3. The *Turanian Family.*

ARYAN OR INDO-EUROPEAN FAMILY.

The Aryas migrated northward and southward of their primitive abode, as is shown by the two divisions indicated in the table, and this migration enables us to determine with a fair degree of certainty the particular spot inhabited by the primitive Aryas.

The Northern Division includes six classes :—1. the *Teutonic*; 2. the *Windic*; 3. the *Hellenic*; 4. the *Illyric*; 5. the *Italic*; and 6. the *Keltic*.

THE TEUTONIC CLASS,

is subdivided into three branches, viz.: the *Low German*, the *Scandinavian*, and the *High German* branches.

The *Low German* branch comprises the *Gothic*, *Old Saxon*, *Old Dutch*, *Old Friesian*, and *Anglo-Saxon*, all of which are now dead; and the *Dutch*, spoken in Holland; the *Friesian*, in *Friesia*; the *Platt Deutsch*, in Lower Germany; and the *English*, spoken by more than a hundred millions of men.

The *Scandinavian* branch includes one dead language —the *Old Norse*—and the living dialects of *Sweden*, *Denmark*, *Norway*, and *Iceland*.

The *High German* branch comprises the *Middle High German* and the *Old High German*, both dead; and the *German* language, now spoken in the greater part of Germany.

THE WINDIC, OR SLAVONIC CLASS,

can also be subdivided into three branches, viz.:—1. the *Lettic*; 2. the *South-Eastern Slavonic*; and 3. the *West Slavonic* branches.

The *Lettic* branch includes the *Lettish*, spoken in Kurland and Livonia; the *Old Prussian*, which has been dead two centuries; and the *Lithuanian*, spoken by some of the inhabitants of Eastern Prussia and of the adjacent frontier of Russia.

Three languages also form the second branch of the *Windic Class*, viz.—The *Illyrian*, which may be regarded as a common name for the *Servian*, the *Croatian* of the *Slovinian* dialects; the *Bulgarian*, and the *Russian*, with its dialects.

To the *West Slavonic branch* belong the *Polish*, the

Bohemian, the *Lusatian,* spoken by the *Wends,* and one dead language—the *Old Bohemian.*

THE HELLENIC CLASS,

which comprises the four dialects of the Classical Greek—*Doric, Æolic, Attic* and *Ionic*—from which have sprung the *Romaic* or *Modern Greek,* and numerous dialects.

THE ILLYRIC CLASS,

only contains one language closely related to the Greek, and called *Albanian.*

THE ITALIC CLASS,

includes Latin and its dialects, viz.—the *Oscan,* spoken south of Rome, and the *Umbrian,* used by the Northern inhabitants of Italy.

It was from these dialects, as well as from the Classical language of Italy, that sprang the *Lingua Vulgaris,* the *Langue d'Oc* and *Langue d'Oil,* now dead, and the *Italian, French, Spanish, Portuguese, Provençal, Wallachian, Romanese,* and *Enghadine* languages.

The *Provençal* was the language of the *Troubadours,* and though still used in the South of France, is a mere *patois,* having lost the literary excellence it had attained.

The *Wallachian,* called also Románia, is spoken in Wallachia, Moldavia, Hungary, Transylvania, and Bessarabia.

The *Romanese* is the language of the Grisons of Switzerland, and the *Enghadine* that of the inhabitants of the Borders of Tyrol.

THE KELTIC CLASS,

is subdivided into two branches, viz.—the *Gadhelic* and the *Kymric* branches.

The first branch comprises the *Scotch,* spoken in the Highlands of Scotland; the *Irish,* almost entirely superseded by the English, and chiefly used by the poorer inhabitants of the South-west of Ireland; and the *Manx,* spoken in the Isle of Man.

The second branch includes the *Armorican,* spoken in Brittany, the *Welsh* in Wales, and the extinct *Cornish.*

The *Southern division* comprises two classes, viz.—the *Indic* and the *Iranic.*

THE INDIC CLASS,

includes the *Sanskrit,* or ancient language of India, the *Hindi, Hindustani, Mahratti, Gudjerati* and *Bengali,* spoken in different parts of India; the *Modern Sanskrit* and the *Páli,* both dead; the *Cinghalese,* used in Ceylon; and the *Zingari,* or language of the Gipsies.

THE IRANIC CLASS,

contains the ancient sacred language of the *Zoroastrians* or *Fire Worshippers* of Persia, viz.—the *Zend.*

It also includes the *Old Armenian,* the language used in the *Cuneiform Inscriptions,* the *Pehlevi* and the *Parsi,* all of which have long been dead languages; the *Persian,* the dialects of *Afghan,* of *Kurdistan,* and of *Bokhara,* the *Armenian* and the *Ossethian,* spoken in the Caucasus.

SEMITIC OR SYRO-ARABIAN FAMILY.

This family is divided into three classes:—

1. The *Aramaic* or *Northern.*

2. The *Hebraic* or *Middle*.
3. The *Arabic* or *Southern*.

THE ARAMAIC OR NORTHERN CLASS,

comprises the *Chaldee, Syriac* and the *Cuneiform Inscriptions of Babylon and Nineveh,* and one living tongue—the *Neo-Syriac*.

THE HEBRAIC, OR MIDDLE,

includes the *Biblical Hebrew,* the *Phœnician Inscriptions,* the *Samaritan,* and the *Carthaginian,* all of which are now dead. To the same class belong also the different dialects now spoken by the Jews.

THE ARABIC, OR SOUTHERN,

comprehends two dead languages—viz., the *Hymyaritic,* the *Ethiopic,* and the *Amharic* or *Abyssinian* of Gondar; the *Sheez* or Abyssinian of Sigre, and the different dialects of the *Arabic* language.

TURANIAN FAMILY.

It includes all the languages which do not belong to either of the two first-named families, with very few exceptions.

The languages belonging to this important family can be separated into two large divisions, viz.:—

1. *A Northern Division.*
2. *A Southern Division.*

The *Northern division* comprehends five classes:

The Tungusic Class,

subdivided into two branches, an *Eastern* and a *Western* one, includes the languages spoken by the Northern inhabitants of China.

The Mongolic Class,

comprises three branches—viz., an *Eastern* branch, a *Northern* one, and a *Western* one; and in it are included all the languages spoken in the Eastern parts of Siberia by the Mongols, the Buriäts, and the Kalmuks.

The Turkic Class,

is divided into *Chagataïc*, *Northern* and *Western* branches. It may be considered as the most important Class of this division of the Turanian family, as the languages that belong to it extend over a considerable portion of the world, from the most remote Northern regions, to the sunny shores of the Adriatic.

The *Osmanli* or *Turkish* language spoken in Europe belongs to this class.

The Samoyedic Class,

is divided into two branches—viz., an *Eastern* branch and a *Northern* one, and comprehends the dialects of the Samoyedes, of the Kamas, of the Urages, and of the Tawgi.

The Finnic Class,

is subdivided into *Chudic*, *Bulgaric*, *Permic*, and *Ugric* classes. The languages of the Chudic branch are spoken by the people of the coasts of the Baltic; those of the

Bulgaric ones by the inhabitants of the banks of the Volga; those of the Permic branch by the Votiakes, the Sirianes, and the Permians; those of the Ugric by the Hungarians, the Voguls, and the Ugro-Ostiakes.

THE SOUTHERN DIVISION,

comprehends five branches—viz., 1. the *Taic*; 2. the *Malaïc*; 3. the *Gangetic*; 3. the *Munda*; 4. the *Lohitic*; and 5. the *Tamulic*.

THE TAIC CLASS,

includes the dialects of Siam, of Laos, and Cambodia.

THE MALAÏC CLASS,

comprises the languages of Polynesia, such as the dialects of Java, Sumatra, Malacca, etc.

THE GANGETIC CLASS,

is divided into *Trans-Himalayan* and *Sub-Himalayan* branches. The languages belonging to this class are spoken in the South-Western part of China, near India.

THE MUNDA CLASS,

includes the dialects of Ho, of Sinhbhum, of Sontal, of Bhumii and Mundala.

THE LOHITIC CLASS,

comprises numerous dialects of Asia, such as those of Khyeng, Kami, Kumi, Shendus, Mru, etc.

The Tamulic Class,

comprehends the *Canarese*, the *Tamil*, the *Telegu*, and the *Malayalam*.

Our genealogical table includes nearly all the languages spoken on the surface of the earth, except a few unclassified ones, such as the *Japanese*—which has however been found to be a member of the Turanian family—the numerous dialects spoken in the Caucasus, the *Chinese*, and the Polysynthetic aboriginal languages of America and South Africa, and also the *Basque* language, spoken in Europe by the inhabitants of the Basque provinces.

ARAMAIC, OR NORTHERN CLASS.

- Chaldee
- Syriac.
- Neo-Syriac.
- Cuneiform Inscriptions of Babylon and Nineveh.

NORTHERN TURKIC CLASS.

Western B.
- Dialects of Rumelia.
- Dialects of Anatolia.
- Dialects of Krimea.
- Dialects of Aderbijan.
- Dialects of Derbend.

Northern B.
- Dialects of the Yakuts.
- Dialects of Siberia.
- Dialects of the Meshcheryaks.
- Dialects of the Karakalpaks.
- Dialects of the Karachais.
- Dialects of the Kumians.
- Dialects of the Nogais.
- Dialects of the Bashkirs.
- Dialects of the Kirgis.

Chagataic B.
- Dialects of Kasan.
- Dialects of the Turkomans.
- Dialects of the Usbeks.
- Dialects of the Chagatais.
- Dialects of the Komans.
- Dialects of the Uigurs.

MONGOLIC

Western B.
- Dialects of the Tokpas.
- Dialects of the Aimaks.
- Dialects of the Dürbet.
- Dialect of the Torgod.
- Dial. of the Dsungur.
- Dialects of the Choschot.

Northern B.
- Dialects of the Buriats.

- Armenian.
- Ossetic
- Dialect of Bhatniar.
- Dialect of Kurdistan.
- Dialect of Afghan.
- Persian.
- Parsi.
- Pehlevi.
- Cuneiform Inscriptions.
- Old Armenian.
- Zend.
- Dialects of the Gipsies or Zingari.
- Pali.
- Cinghalese.
- Modern Sanskrit.
- Bengali.
- Gudjerati.
- Mahratti.
- Hindustani.
- Hindi.
- Vedic Sanskrit.

	ARABIC, OR SOUTHERN CLASS.
	- Hymyaritic Inscriptions. - Ethiopic. - Amharic. - Dialect of Arabic. - Ghez.

	HEBRAIC, OR MIDDLE CLASS.
	- Carthaginian. - Dialects of the Jews. - Samaritan. - Phœnician Inscriptions. - Biblical Hebrew.

DIVISION.

MUNDA CLASS.
- Dialects of Ho.
- Dialects of Sinhbhum.
- Dialects of Sontal.
- Dialects of Bhumij.
- Dialects of Munda.la.

GANGETIC CLASS.

Himalayan B.
- Dialect of Chepang.
- Dialects of Newar.
- Dialect of Murmi.
- Dialects of Limbu.
- Dialects of Kiranti.
- Dialects of Lepcha.
- Dialect of Tenaveri.
- Dialect of Sarpa.

Trans-Himalayan B.
- Dialect of Tibetan.
- Dialect of Harpa.
- Dialect of Tâh-Sifan.
- Dialect of Takpa.
- Dialect of Manyak-Sifan.
- Dialect of Gyarung-Sifan.

LOHITIC
- Dialects of Sibsagor.
- Dialect of Abor.
- Dialects of Abor-Miri.
- Dialects of Mira.
- Dialect of Burmese.
- Dialects of Deoli.
- Dialects of Kachari-Bodo.
- Dialect of Garo.
- Dialects of Changlo.
- Dialect of Mikir.
- Dialects of Dhimal.

14, *Henrietta Street, Covent Garden, London;* and
20, *South Frederick Street, Edinburgh.*

WILLIAMS AND NORGATE'S
LIST OF
French, German, Italian, Latin, and Greek,
AND OTHER
SCHOOL BOOKS AND MAPS.

French.
FOR PUBLIC SCHOOLS WHERE LATIN IS TAUGHT.

Eugène (G.) The Student's Comparative Grammar of the French Language, with an Historical Sketch of the Formation of French. For the use of Public Schools. With Exercises. 2nd Improved Edition. Square crown 8vo, cloth. 5s.
Or Grammar, 3s.; Exercises, 2s. 6d.

"The appearance of a Grammar like this is in itself a sign that great advance is being made in the teaching of modern as well as of ancient languages..... The rules and observations are all scientifically classified and explained..... Mr. Eugène's book is one that we can strongly recommend for use in the higher forms of large schools."—*Educational Times.*

"In itself this is in many ways the most satisfactory Grammar for beginners that we have as yet seen..... The book is likely to be useful to all who wish either to learn or to teach the French language."—*Athenæum.*

Eugène's French Method. Elementary French Lessons. Easy Rules and Exercises preparatory to the "Student's Comparative French Grammar." By the same Author. 2nd Edition. Crown 8vo, cloth. 1s. 6d.

"Certainly deserves to rank among the best of our Elementary French Exercise-books."—*Educational Times.*

"To those who begin to study French, I may recommend, as the best book of the kind with which I am acquainted, '*Eugène's Elementary Lessons in French.*' It is only after having fully mastered this small manual and Exercise-book that they ought to begin the more systematic study of French."—*Dr. Breymann, Lecturer of the French Language and Literature, Owen's College, Manchester (Preface to Philological French Grammar).*

Eugène's Comparative French-English Studies, Grammatical and Idiomatic. Being a Second, entirely re-written, Edition of the "French Exercises for Middle and Upper Forms." Cloth. 2s. 6d.

Attwell (H.) Twenty Supplementary French Lessons, with Etymological Vocabularies. Chiefly for the use of Schools where Latin is taught. Crown 8vo, cloth. 2s.

Krueger (H.) Short French Grammar. 4th Edition. 180 pp. 12mo, cloth. 2s.

Eugène (G.) French Irregular Verbs scientifically classified with constant Reference to Latin. Reprinted from his Grammar. 8vo, sewed. 6d.

Ahn's French Familiar Dialogues, and French-English Vocabulary for English Schools. 12mo, cloth. 2s.

Brasseur (Prof. Isid.) Grammar of the French Language, comprehending New and complete Rules on the Genders of French Nouns. 20th Edition. 12mo, cloth. 3s. 6d.

—— Key to the French Grammar. 12mo, cloth. 3s.

—— Selection from Chesterfield's and Cowper's Letters, with Notes for translating. 5th Edition. 12mo, cloth. 3s.

—— Key. Partie Française du Choix des Lettres. 12mo, cloth. 3s. 6d.

—— Manuel des Ecoliers. A French Reading Book, preceded by Rules on French Pronunciation. 6th Edition. 12mo. 2s. 6d.

—— Premières Lectures. An easy French Reading Book for Children and Beginners. 18mo, cloth. 1s. 6d.

Roche (A.) Nouvelle Grammaire Française. Nouvelle Edition. 12mo, boards. 1s.

Williams (T. S.) and J. Lafont. French and Commercial Correspondence. A Collection of Modern Mercantile Letters in French and English, with their translation on opposite pages. 2nd Edition. 12mo, cloth. 4s. 6d.

For a German Version of the same Letters, vide p. 4.

Fleury's Histoire de France, racontée à la Jeunesse, edited for the use of English Pupils, with Grammatical Notes, by Auguste Beljame, Bachelier-ès-lettres de l'Université de Paris. 2nd Edition. 12mo, cloth boards. 3s. 6d.

Mandrou (A.) Album Poétique de la Jeunesse. A Collection of French Poetry, selected expressly for English Schools by A. Mandrou, M.A. de l'Académie de Paris, Professor of French in the Clergy Orphan School, St. Peter's Collegiate School, the Crystal Palace, &c. 12mo, cloth. 3s. 6d.

German.

Weisse's Complete Practical Grammar of the German Language, with Exercises on Conversations, Letters, Poems and Treatises, &c. 3rd Edition, very much improved. 12mo, cloth. 6s.

────── New Conversational Exercises in German Composition, with complete Rules and Directions, with full References to his German Grammar. 2nd Edition. 12mo, cloth. 3s. 6d.

Schlutter's German Class Book. A Course of Instruction based on Becker's System, and so arranged as to exhibit the Self-development of the Language, and its Affinities with the English. By Fr. Schlutter, Royal Military Academy, Woolwich. 3rd Edition. 12mo, cloth. 5s.

Möller (A.) A German Reading Book. A Companion to Schlutter's German Class Book. With a complete Vocabulary. 150 pp. 12mo, cloth. 2s.

Wittich's German Grammar. 7th Edition. 12mo, cloth. 6s. 6d.

────── German for Beginners. New Edition. 12mo, cloth. 5s.

────── Key to ditto. 12mo, cloth. 7s.

────── German Tales for Beginners, arranged in Progressive Order. 20th Edition. Crown 8vo, cloth. 6s.

Ravensberg (A. v.) Practical Grammar of the German Language. Conversational Exercises, Dialogues and Idiomatic Expressions. 2 vols. in 1. 12mo, cloth. 5s.

────── Key to the Exercises. Cloth. 2s.

────── Rose's English into German. A Selection of Anecdotes, Stories, Portions of Comedies, &c., with copious Notes for Translation into English. By A. v. Ravensberg. 2nd Edition. 2 Parts in 1. Cloth. 4s. 6d.

────── Key to Rose's English into German. Cloth. 5s.

────── German Reader, Prose and Poetry, with copious Notes for Beginners. 2nd Edition. Crown 8vo, cloth. 3s.

────── Student's First Year's German Companion. A concise Conversational Method for Beginners. 12mo, cloth. 2s. 6d.

Sonnenschein and Stallybrass. German for the English. Part I. First Reading Book. Easy Poems with interlinear Translations, and illustrated by Notes and Tables, chiefly Etymological. 4th Edition. 12mo, cloth. 4s. 6d.

Ahn's German Method by Rose. A New Edition of the genuine Book, with a Supplement consisting of Models of Conjugations, a Table of all Regular Dissonant and Irregular Verbs, Rules on the Prepositions, &c. &c. By A. V. Rose. 2 Courses in 1 vol. Cloth. 3s. 6d.

—————— German Method by Rose, &c. First Course. Cloth. 2s.

Apel's Short and Practical German Grammar for Beginners, with copious Examples and Exercises. 2nd Edition. 12mo; cloth. 2s. 6d.

[Black's] Thieme's Complete Grammatical German Dictionary, in which are introduced the Genitives and Plurals and other Irregularities of Substantives, the Comparative Degrees of Adjectives, and the Irregularities of Verbs. Square 8vo, strongly bound. 6s.

Koehler (F.) German-English and English-German Dictionary. 2 vols. 1120 pp., treble columns, royal 8vo, in one vol., half-bound. 9s.

Williams (T. S.) Modern German and English Conversations and Elementary Phrases, the German revised and corrected by A. Kokemueller. 21st enlarged and improved Edition. 12mo, cloth. 3s. 6d.

—————— and C. Cruse. German and English Commercial Correspondence. A Collection of Modern Mercantile Letters in German and English, with their Translation on opposite pages. 12mo, cloth. 4s. 6d.

For a French Version of the same Letters, vide p. 2.

Apel (M.) German Prose Stories for Beginners (including Lessing's Prose Fables), with an interlinear Translation in the natural order of Construction. 12mo, cloth. 2s. 6d.

—————— German Poetry. A Collection of German Poetry for the use of Schools and Families, containing nearly 300 Pieces selected from the Works of 70 different Authors. Crown 8vo, cloth. 5s.

—————— German Prose. A Collection of the best Specimens of German Prose, chiefly from Modern Authors. A Handbook for Schools and Families. 500 pp. Crown 8vo, cloth. 3s.

Andersen (H. C.) Bilderbuch Ohne Bilder. The German Text, with Explanatory Notes, &c., and a complete Vocabulary, for the use of Schools, by Alphons Beck. 12mo, cloth limp. 2s.

Chamisso's Peter Schlemihl. The German Text, with copious Explanatory Notes and a Vocabulary, by M. Förster. Crown 8vo, cloth. 2s.

Goethe's Hermann und Dorothea. With Grammatical and Explanatory Notes and a complete Vocabulary, by M. Förster. 12mo, cloth. 2s. 6d.

——— **Hermann und Dorothea.** With Grammatical Notes by A. von Ravensberg. Crown 8vo, cloth. 2s. 6d.

——— **Hermann und Dorothea.** The German Text, with corresponding English Hexameters on opposite pages. By F. B. Watkins, M.A., Professor of Greek and Latin, Queen's College, Liverpool. Crown 8vo, cloth. 3s.

——— **Egmont.** The German Text, with Explanatory Notes and a complete Vocabulary, by H. Apel. 12mo, cloth. 2s. 6d.

——— **Faust.** With copious Notes by Falk Lebahn. 8vo, cloth. 10s. 6d.

Goldschmidt (H. E.) German Poetry. A Selection of the best Modern Poems, with the best English Translations on opposite pages. Crown 8vo, cloth. 5s.

Hauff's Mærchen. A Selection from Hauff's Fairy Tales. The German Text, with a Vocabulary in foot-notes. By A. Hoare, B.A. Crown 8vo, cloth. 3s. 6d.

Nieritz. Die Waise, a German Tale, with numerous Explanatory Notes for Beginners, and a complete Vocabulary, by E. C. Otte. 12mo, cloth. 2s. 6d.

Carové (J. W.) Mæhrchen ohne Ende (The Story without an End). 12mo, cloth. 2s.

Lessing's Minna von Barnhelm, the German Text, with Explanatory Notes for translating into English, and a complete Vocabulary, by J. A. F. Schmidt. 12mo, cloth. 2s. 6d.

Schiller's Song of the Bell, German Text, with English Poetical Translation on the opposite pages, by J. Hermann Merivale, Esq. 12mo, cloth. 1s.

Fouque's Undine, Sintram, Aslauga's Ritter, die beiden Hauptleute. 4 vols. in 1. 8vo, cloth. 7s. 6d.

Undine. 1s. 6d.; cloth, 2s.   Aslauga. 1s. 6d.; cloth, 2s.
Sintram. 2s. 6d.; cloth, 3s.   Hauptleute. 1s. 6d.; cloth, 2s.

Latin and Greek.

Jessopp (Rev. Dr.) Manual of Greek Accidence. New Edition. Crown 8vo. 3s. 6d.

Bryce (Rev. Dr.) The Laws of Greek Accentuation Simplified. 3rd Edition, with the most essential Rules of Quantity. 12mo, sewed. 6d.

Euripides' Medea. The Greek Text, with Introduction and Explanatory Notes for Schools, by J. H. Hogan. 8vo, cloth. 3s. 6d.

—— Ion. Greek Text, with Notes for Beginners, Introduction and Questions for Examination, by the Rev. Charles Badham, D.D. 2nd Edition. 8vo. 3s. 6d.

Æschylus. Agamemnon. Revised Greek Text, with literal line-for-line Translation on opposite pages, by John F. Davies, B.A. 8vo, cloth. 3s.

Platonis Philebus. With Introduction and Notes by Dr. C. Badham. 2nd Edition, considerably augmented. 8vo, cloth. 4s.

—— Euthydemus et Laches. With Critical Notes and an Epistola critica to the Senate of the Leyden University, by the Rev. Ch. Badham, D.D. 8vo, cloth. 4s.

—— Symposium, and Letter to the Master of Trinity, "De Platonis Legibus,"—Platonis Convivium, cum Epistola ad Thompsonum edidit Carolus Badham. 8vo, cloth. 4s.

Sophocles. Electra. The Greek Text critically revised, with the aid of MSS. newly collated and explained. By Rev. H. F. M. Blaydes, M.A., formerly Student of Christ Church, Oxford. 8vo, cloth. 6s.

—— Philoctetes. Edited by the same. 8vo, cloth. 6s.

—— Trachiniæ. Edited by the same. 8vo, cloth. 6s.

—— Ajax. Edited by the same. 8vo, cloth. 6s.

Kiepert's New Atlas Antiquus. Maps of the Ancient World, for Schools and Colleges. 6th Edition. With a complete Geographical Index. Folio, boards. 7s. 6d.

—— The same, without the Index. 6s. 6d.

Italian.

Volpe (Cav. G.) Eton Latin Grammar, for the use of Eton College. Including Exercises and Examples. New Edition. Crown 8vo, cloth. 4s. 6d.
—— Key to the Exercises. 1s.
Rossetti. Exercises for securing Idiomatic Italian by means of Literal Translations from the English, by Maria F. Rossetti. 12mo, cloth. 3s. 6d.
—— Aneddoti Italiani. One Hundred Italian Anecdotes, selected from "Il Compagno del Passeggio." Being also a Key to Rossetti's Exercises. 12mo, cloth. 2s. 6d.

Danish—Dutch.

Bojesen (Mad. Marie) The Danish Speaker. Pronunciation of the Danish Language, Vocabulary, Dialogues and Idioms for the use of Students and Travellers in Denmark and Norway. 12mo, cloth. 4s.
Rask (E.) Danish Grammar for Englishmen. With Extracts in Prose and Verse. 2nd Edition. Edited by Repp. 8vo. 5s.
Ferrall, Repp, and Rosing. Danish-English and English-Danish Dictionary. New Edition. 2 Parts in 1. Square 8vo. 14s.
Williams and Ludolph. Dutch and English Dialogues, and Elementary Phrases. 12mo. 2s. 6d.

Wall Maps.

Sydow's Wall Maps of Physical Geography for School-rooms, representing the purely physical proportions of the Globe, drawn on a very large scale. An English Edition, the Originals with English Names and Explanations. Mounted on canvas, with rollers:
  1. The World. 12 Sheets. Mounted. 10s.
  2. Europe. 9 Sheets. Mounted. 10s.
  3. Asia. 9 Sheets. Mounted. 10s.
  4. Africa. 6 Sheets. 10s.
  5. America (North and South). 2 Maps, 10 Sheets. 10s.
  6. Australia and Australasia. 6 Sheets. Mounted. 10s.
—— Handbook to the Series of Large Physical Maps for School Instruction, edited by J. Tilleard. 8vo. 1s.

Miscellaneous.

De Rheims (H.). Practical Lines in Geometrical Drawing, containing the Use of Mathematical Instruments and the Construction of Scales, the Elements of Practical and Descriptive Geometry, Orthographic and Horizontal Projections, Isometrical Drawing and Perspective. Illustrated with 300 Diagrams, and giving (by analogy) the solution of every Question proposed at the Competitive Examinations for the Army. 8vo, cloth. 9s.

Fuerst's Hebrew Lexicon, by Davidson. A Hebrew and Chaldee Lexicon to the Old Testament, by Dr. Julius Fuerst. 4th Edition, improved and enlarged, containing a Grammatical and Analytical Appendix. Translated by Rev. Dr. Samuel Davidson. 1600 pp., royal 8vo, cloth. 21s.

Hebrew Texts. Large type. 16mo, cloth. each 1s.
 The Book of Genesis. 1s.
 The Psalms. 1s.
 The Book of Job. 1s.
 The Prophet Isaiah. 1s.

Attwell (Prof. H.) Table of Aryan (Indo-European) Languages, showing their Classification and Affinities, with copious Notes; to which is added, Grimm's Law of the Interchange of Mute Consonants, with numerous Illustrations. A Wall Map for the use of Colleges and Lecture-rooms. 2nd Edition. Mounted with rollers. 10s.

——— The same Table, in 4to, with numerous Additions. Boards. 7s. 6d.

Williams and Simmonds. English Commercial Correspondence. A Collection of Modern Mercantile Letters. By T. S. Williams and P. L. Simmonds, Author of "A Dictionary of Trade Products," Editor of "The Technologist." 12mo, cloth. 4s.

Bayldon. Icelandic Grammar. An Elementary Grammar of the Old Norse or Icelandic Language. By Rev. George Bayldon. 8vo, cloth. 7s. 6d.

Small's Handbook of Sanskrit Literature. Compiled from the best Authorities by the Rev. G. Small, formerly Missionary at Calcutta and Benares. Intended specially for the use of Candidates for the Indian Civil Service. Crown 8vo, cloth. 6s.